MW01028936

CRACK THE CODE

THE WHOLE BOOK
RIGHT HERE

- **SUCCESS IS OURS.** Of course, we'll graduate! Of course, we belong in college. Our story is our choice. We must be the author of the story on which we build our future.

- **ASK.** It's okay not to know. It's not okay not to ask. Some peers and professors won't speak in ways that are familiar or comfortable. Never mind—they're just new to this, like we are. Just ask direct questions often and clarify the answers.

- **HAVE ALL KINDS OF FRIENDS.** Friends who share our experiences are life supports. Friends with different experiences let us learn about unfamiliar worlds so we can become comfortable there.

- **MENTAL HEALTH IS KEY.** Hard work matters, but healthy behaviors and relaxing activities actually help us tap into our most productive selves. Mental health is key to our academic and life success.

- **RESTRICT POVERTY TO MONEY.** It sucks to be poor but the reason we are in college is so we don't have to be poor always. Learning money management while we don't have much is very helpful for when we have more.

- **BE CAREFUL OF "SUPPOSED TO."** It is so much easier to do the things that we want to do, rather than the things other people think we should do. Classes get much easier when they are about topics that interest us.

- **CHOOSE CURIOSITY OVER JUDGMENT.** It's natural to group people by the way they look or sound; it's hard to figure out why people are who they are. Yet, if we don't take the time to do it for others, can we expect others to do it for us?

> First Generation students come from families where their biological parents did not complete a four-year college degree.

- **FAIL FORWARD.** Sometimes we meet failure, so fail forward. Learn from the failure. Take what failure teaches to tack toward success.

- **HAVE A SCHEDULE.** Routines. Routines. Routines. Recognize your biological clock and find a doable schedule for sleeping, working, going to class, chilling. An every-day routine beats random planning.

- **SMALL STEPS FOR BIG GAINS.** When overwhelmed, it helps to break tasks down into small chunks and look for the learning style that works best for us. There isn't one right way.

- **TAKE IN ALL COLLEGE CAN OFFER.** College is as much about what happens outside the classroom as what happens in class. Use student organizations, summer experiences, traveling, networking and the work you do for money to help with the classroom-to-career transition. After all, college graduation isn't as far off as it may feel.

CRACK THE CODE

A GUIDE TO COLLEGE SUCCESS FOR FIRST GENS

Susan Abel Lieberman

A print version of **Crack the Code** is available on Amazon.
While reading the book in print form, you may wish also to
download the free PDF, available on the book's website and use
it to open the links cited in the book with just one click.

www.FirstGenCollegeSuccess

*(In the PDF, when you put your cursor over a link,
a small box with a down pointing arrow will appear at
the end of the line. Click on it and the link will open.)*

For additional information email **susan@lieberman.net**

If you find this Guide of value, it would be terrific if you would
make a brief video about the book, and post it on the website.
There are instructions on how to do this easily on the site.

TABLE OF CONTENTS

HOW THIS BOOK CAME TO BE

FIRST I MET LA' SHAYE

This book might not exist if I hadn't met La'Shaye Cobley at VerdeXchange, a conference on green technology in Los Angeles. My brother runs this conference every year, and I thought I would show up for the fifth anniversary. At an early coffee break, I saw a young Black woman standing alone, off to one side. I know nothing about green or tech, so, understandably, no one was interested in talking to me, and no one seemed interested in talking with her either.

I walked over to chat. We clicked. Turns out she has just the sort of story that grabs my attention. She grew up in a low-income, minority neighborhood in Brooklyn and won a full scholarship to Bowdoin, a small private liberal arts college in Maine. She went on to earn a Ph.D. in ecology at the University of Utah and is now working for the California Air Resources Board. Having mentored under-resourced minority students for decades, I was interested in her experiences and thoughts about how she has gotten to now.

I have written ten books, and all of them might generally fall into the advice-book category. The last book I wrote was *How to Find Good Work Without a College Degree.* The minute La'Shaye said she wanted to write a book for First Generation (First Gen) students; I vibrated. I knew I wanted to do it as well. I had the time and skills, and she had the immediate life experiences and insights. There, in those coffee breaks at the conference, we decided, hardly knowing each other but working from instinct and intuition, to undertake this project together. Before we left the conference, we agreed we would write the book, put it up on Amazon as cheaply as they would let us, and take no profit if it happened there was some.

THEN LA'SHAYE HAD TO STOP, BUT I COULD NOT

I, retired with few responsibilities, went home to work on the book. La'Shaye went back to a demanding work schedule. Then the Coronavirus hit. I had more time and she had more pressures. Finally, sadly, we agreed that this was not her time to work on a book, but I was unstoppable. Her advice and ideas gave me impetus and focus.

FIFTY YEARS OF FIRST GEN CONNECTIONS CAME INTO FOCUS

I grew up privileged, but always with a strong connection to the First Gen world. My first serious love, as an undergraduate at Berkeley, was Ron Serrano, a Mexican American First Generation college student who started at Cal Tech. He found it unhospitable and transferred to UC Berkley to get an engineering degree with a focus on water desalination. We planned to drive to LA to meet his parents the spring break of our senior year. That trip was cancelled when he had a cerebral aneurysm the night before we were to leave, dying 12 days later. I met his parents at the hospital.

Since college, I have been deeply involved in mentorship programs and interacted with scores of students in under-resourced high schools. Five of those students I was able to support intimately on their journey through college.

Stephanie was the niece of our babysitter, Dolly Fletcher. When Dolly was dying, she asked me to promise to help Steph get to college. Stephanie taught me a graduate degree's worth of learning about the challenges of going off to college with no money, no support, no preparation, and no clue. Now she's a lawyer.

In writing *How to Thrive and Survive in High School*, I did focus groups at an inner-city high school and met Tram who came from Vietnam with no English and now has a master's degree in finance. Her friend—now husband—came as an outstanding college chemistry student but without computer or English skills. Switching to math, he now teaches at the community college, especially kids who come deficient in math.

The high school counselor also asked me to work with Jose, a bright Latino who had given up on school because, he said, "I have no future." He was, he slowly revealed, undocumented. Nonetheless, he graduated from the University of Houston with an engineering degree. Sadly, his immigration status has stood in the way of him working as an electrical engineer.

For two decades I have had the satisfaction of watching Elisabeth, a powerful Latino woman, grow from an unsure high school student to a tenured associate professor at a major university. And now I find myself learning from Cristal and her husband. We began working together when we were matched through a program called Project Grad. I have also gotten to know her husband who was in a rut with just a GED. Now he is in his second year of technical college. I think they will say I have been helpful to them, but learning from their struggles and watching their resilience for the past three years has been a gift to me.

I may have been a mentor to each of these people, but they have also been my teachers. I have never walked in their shoes, but in walking with them, I was allowed to see into their lives and appreciate their struggles. They are inspiring. It is my good fortune that they have trusted me to be part of their lives.

ADVICE AND WISDOM FROM ALL OVER

I needed to hear many more voices of First Generation college students from all kinds of backgrounds studying in all kinds of situations. At first, I thought I could interview a hundred students on my own. In time, I decided I would hear at least a hundred voices, but I didn't have to interview all of them in person.

I did hold 60 phone conversations with First Generation students or recent graduates that I found by networking my way around the country. I relied on contacts with people I already know and branched out, tapping their networks. I asked every student I interviewed if he or she could connect me with First Gen friends. The interview sample is random. It is weighted toward Texans since I spent 30 years in Houston and toward San Diegoans where I now live. At one top ten school, I ended up with five interviews. I enjoyed those thoughtful conversations so much that I was moved to write their school president a note. I did not try to balance gender or ethnicity, just eagerly took what came my way.

Most interviews were about an hour. Some conversations lasted more than two hours. With only one exception, they were deeply interesting and informative for me. The kindness, thoughtfulness, and insights of these students made this book possible.

I searched the web to find other stories embedded in websites focused on First Gens, including the videos of students from the University of Nevada at Reno. Thanks to the Trio program at Indiana University Purdue-Fort Wayne, I read 55 personal essays from First Generation students published in two volumes titled, *Every Student Has a Story*. The 25 student voices quoted in Abraham Jack's book, *Privileged Poor*, increased my understanding of challenges facing students at an elite university.

I also talked with faculty and administrators who are involved in helping First Gen students navigate college successfully, although they were more difficult to access and less willing to help than the students, and I'm still not sure why. Those who were themselves the first in their families to go to college and found their own experiences repeated a decade or two later were especially valuable.

As the text was coming toward completion, and I was fretting about how to ask people to find time to read and critique a hundred pages, Dr. Haliday Douglas had an inspired suggestion: "Let's put together a book club of relevant readers and ask them to tackle chunks each week over six to eight weeks." And that's what happened. Haliday facilitated these zoom conversations with three people who are involved in college prep programs, two current First Generation students and three graduates. Many others read sections along the way. This is a better book because of their generous work; their contributions were enormously helpful.

FIRST GEN VOICES

Most of the quotes in this book are as they were told to me but lightly edited from handwritten notes. In a few cases, similar thoughts of two people are combined in one quote. In every instance, I have aimed to be true to the intention and spirit of the interviewees. Although I am the only author, you will find I use *we* instead of *I* in most of the text. That's because, truly, it is a collaborative effort. The book comes from all who contributed. If I am the glue, everyone else is the glitter.

To all who helped write this book by talking with me, THANK YOU! You are the inspiration, motivation, information, and insight. As importantly, you brought such joyfulness into my life—and most of it came while I was sequestered because of Covid-19. That was a grand gift.

That you thought this work was important and wanted to be part of it made the task a privilege. As I promised confidentiality in my phone interviews, I did not use the real names of interviewees in the book, and so I do not identify you here, but this book could not exist without you. I hope I have lived up to your expectations. I take full responsibility for any errors, mistakes or accidental stupidities.

1

INTRODUCTION

A GUIDE TO HELP AND ENCOURAGE STUDENTS EMBRACING COLLEGE

Getting to college is complicated. Turns out that going to college is also complicated . . . and exciting . . . important . . . life changing. Also, according to the sixty-plus First Generation students interviewed, it's sometimes scary . . . challenging . . . joyous . . . hard . . . and more.

If you were planning a big cross-country trip, it would help to know which roads are unsafe, where you can find car repairs, good places to stop for rest and relaxation, and what things you absolutely must see. This is that guide to help you with the challenges of going on your First Generation[1] college student adventure. It gives you the experiences and wisdom of First Gens who have gone before you and shares what they wished they had known earlier.

While there are many ways to design a good life, this book is directed specifically at students who have chosen to embrace the decision to go to college. It rests on the belief that college, while not the only avenue forward, is a place that can provide us with tools to take control of our lives and make informed choices. Life keeps serving up new questions. The hope is that your experiences in college will equip you with the skills and resources—intellectual, emotional and tangible—to work out good answers.

---

1   See Appendix III for a discussion of how colleges define "First Generation."

It would be great if all students went off to college with an invisible mentor tucked into their backpacks, ready to whisper advice, helpful hints, and important warnings in their ears as they took their college trip. That kind of magic could make life easier, more fun, and less stressful for so many students. This Guide aims to approximate that magic mentor, unseen guide, wise friend beside you.

There is no single formula for being a successful college student, no straight line from *Go* to *Graduate*. In these pages, you will find students at community colleges and students at Ivy League institutions; people working their way through school with barely enough money for gas and people with full scholarships—and they all have felt the weight of being a First Generation student. They all speak of their challenges, struggles, failures, and successes.

Every person interviewed, regardless of the story, said that being a First Generation college student was A THING, an awareness that made them feel they came to college with a few extra rocks in their backpacks. These First Gen students often faced systemic struggles with institutions not fully appreciative of their backgrounds; they want to become a community of support for you. As different as the single mother who failed out of college twice before graduating is from the University of California aerospace engineer on the dean's list, they shared common feelings, fears, and hopes for their futures.

We each have our own unique identity. That identity makes you special. However crazy your life might sometimes seem to you, there are strengths, lessons, perceptions, experiences that you bring to the rest of us. Others can learn from you, as you can learn from them.

Yes, this book is meant to help you do well in college, but, as importantly, it is meant to help you get comfortable and contented in your own skin because that makes going to school easier. All of us come from a community; our identity is a product of that community. Then, at college we find we need to develop a new, supportive community. It may sometimes feel like you are in an amusement park on the roller coaster. You are riding up, you are plummeting down, you are seeing things at lightning speed, and maybe you worry about throwing up; you are laughing—or is it screaming—and then, you are rolling back to where you started, not quite the same as when you bought your ticket.

Just as the city engineers put up signs to keep pedestrians from walking into potholes and breaking bones, the intention of this book is to help you navigate successfully. Your success benefits the entire community. Many First Generation students who have eagerly lent their voices did so because . . . *"I would have so loved to have a book like this."*

TAKE ACTION

Take a minute to look at the Table of Contents. Think about the questions most on your mind now and decide if you want to begin reading somewhere in the middle. Know there is a Glossary at the end if you find a word that puzzles you. **Also check the index to find topics of interest quickly.**

If it is before the start of your freshman year, contact your college and ask if there is a before-school orientation program or a freshman year program for First Gen students. Find out how you can participate.

ROLLING WITH THE PUNCHES: ANTICIPATE AND DODGE

Some issues are common to all college students. That doesn't mean they aren't challenging for you, but the challenges are not because of background, income or personal characteristics.

Here is a list of ten reasons where students from all backgrounds get derailed:[2]

✗ TIME MANAGEMENT
✗ DEBT
✗ SPREADING ONESELF TOO THIN
✗ HOMESICKNESS
✗ DEPRESSION
✗ SICKNESS/HEALTH
✗ SOCIAL PROBLEMS
✗ PARTYING TOO MUCH
✗ RELATIONSHIPS
✗ CHOOSING A MAJOR

College stretches everybody—period. However, when racism, poverty, classism, and inadequate preparation are folded in— well, yes it gets more complicated. So, we send you a mixed message. We want to acknowledge that your circumstances as a First Generation student can cause particular problems. But we also want to reassure you that some of what you feel, lots of others from very different backgrounds also feel.

2 https://owlcation.com/academia/common-problems-for-college-students

There is such a laundry list of feelings that come with being the first in your family to go to college—elation, fear, pride, doubt, excitement, curiosity, hesitation, confusion. . . . Whatever you feel, know one thing: It will change. Where you start is not where you will end up. If you arrive on campus overwhelmed by a sense of cluelessness, you will not feel clueless when you graduate. If you arrive floating on a cloud of self-confidence, well, damn, it's likely that you will take some direct hits, too.

There is one course that every college student takes, but it never shows up on any transcript. It's called CHANGE. No grade, just pass/fail. And if you fail, you get to keep taking it. Oh, if you pass, you keep taking it again, too.

Jeep is a guy who never expected to end up in college, and once he got there, he knew no one was waiting with a plan for his life. He was going to have to write it. In a speech to new high school grads, he said, *"There's no Wikipedia about your life out there. You are the one who decides how to write your story."* In the TAKE ACTION section following is his advice.

TAKE ACTION

Choose three events in your life that you feel have impacted you more than anything else. Is there a way to look at things that have felt bad and change that around to see some and/or look at good things and see how they might help your script going forward?

So many First Generation students use the same words to describe college, especially the early months: *"It was so hard . . . being a First Generation student makes everything harder . . ."* This Guide can't make hard things easy, but with the insights of those who went ahead of you, we hope it can make some things easier. You may not need or want to know all of it from the start of college, but as you move forward, different sections may feel more relevant. Read it from front to back or any other way that works for you. Bend the pages, write *notes to self*, look for issues on your mind. Share it with others. Yell at it if you disagree.

TAKE ACTION

Take a minute to think about what you are feeling about going to college. Are you caught up by feelings that might get in the way of your well-being? If you doubt whether you belong in college, make a list of all the reasons you are supposed to be there.

If you know you are in the right place, just jot down things that you worry could get in your way and be looking, as you read on, for how to handle minor roadblocks.

2

THINK ABOUT HOW YOU WANT TO MEASURE SUCCESS

THE WHO AM I? CHALLENGE   10

THE WHO AM I? CHALLENGE

Val, the son of immigrants in Texas, first won a scholarship to an elite boarding school on the west coast and then a full ride to a top ten university on the east coast. He was a neuroscience pre-med who graduated with a 3.3 GPA while working 20 hours or more every year of college and being engaged in campus activities. Trouble was, wanting others to be dazzled did not help him feel good about his life. *"I do this thing where I want to seem impressive, which is why I stayed with my major. Only now have I gotten to the point where I'm done throwing myself at something just because other people will be impressed."* **The loudest message he says this book should send? Figure out who you are and what makes sense for you and not do things to impress or please others.**

This advice was echoed again and again by First Gen students. Fernando let the belief that he had to have a highly lucrative career for his family drive choices that made him dissatisfied. Now that Cecilia is happily engaged in counseling, she deeply regrets that she stuck with political science classes she disliked because her father thought she should be a lawyer. *"At my school,* she said, *"there was a stigma attached to education and liberal arts. Supposedly, they were too easy, and I didn't want to seem weak."* Anna learned that when studying the things that interested her, her classes stopped feeling hard. Savannah spent a decade *"chasing the money."* She wants to tell you not to make her mistake.

You may think, like Khalid, that you are meant to be a surgeon, only to find out you really are a public health activist. Maybe you start out thinking you are a party person, and when you land on academic probation like Trevor, you discover you are— previously unsuspected—someone who can be a first-rate student and chooses to go to graduate school. Because Jeep made a stupid mistake in high school, he thought the world was always going to see him as a felon stuck in a low-level job. Turns out, today he is a well-compensated media expert on his way to an MBA with a full scholarship.

Their message is not that every class, every choice, every job has to delight you. Lots of times, students did things that were not ideal to help reach their goals. They took the exasperating chem class, worked the dispiriting cashier job, pushed for the better grade—to get where they wanted to go. **The problem is when you push to get some place you really won't care about when you arrive.**

Yes, if you grew up without enough money for the bills and know your family would benefit from your financial success, if you have thousands of dollars of debt, if you are tired of being broke, it makes sense to think about post-college earnings. Everybody in our interview cohort had jobs they didn't particularly love to help them get by, and they don't regret those. **But not one person argues that you should work toward a career based only on earnings or the expectations of others**. It was such a big theme in the conversations. (See more about this in Chapter 7, **Money)**

Of course, we use normal external measures to decide if we are successful: Grades, money, clothes, cars, the opinions of friends and family, awards, status. If we hit the mark we set for ourselves, we feel successful. That's normative, but many of the interviewees and much in the research literature encourage you to think of success using internal as well as external measures.

Interviewees with all sorts of stories talk about how failure can also be a measure of success. Daring to take a chance—to do something that feels difficult or challenging—is absolutely a measure of success. But suppose you take that chance—and you fail? You get a bad grade, you speak up and are sure you sounded stupid, you make a commitment and then, in fear, run away from it? If that happens to you, and you stand in front of the mirror, talk to yourself, figure out what you can learn from the experience and go back and try again, well, lots of applause for you. Mustering that kind of determination is certainly a mark of success.

Farrah believes she had a successful college experience because she always showed up curious.

 I got to go to Israel when I was in high school, thanks to this incredible summer opportunities advisor who pushed me into it. What does a Black Christian woman do in Israel? It was so weird, and I just wanted to understand. It was where I learned how much better curiosity is than criticism. Because of that summer, I came to college with a YES mindset. It was a shock to find classmates who were not serious about learning or not connected to the community. I wondered why, and I made up my mind just to be me and engage with people just as I am.

Quentin, who sometimes struggled with tough classes and is now in law school, told us:

 My roommates were all smarter than me and could get better grades working less. But they were just there to make things better for themselves. I was there to make things better for others. I felt I represented all the other young Black students behind me, and I had better make this work for them. Besides, they might be smarter, but they weren't funny and didn't know how to socialize. I decided I get points for that.

Quentin says if he were to go back to his magnet high school and speak to seniors he would say:

Only you can decide what you are going to do. Don't do things that you know do not make you happy. I thought I should be like my mentor and major in economics. It isn't me, but it took a painful semester to figure that out. Explore, pay attention to your passions, and trust your own feelings. You don't have to be the smartest or fastest. You just have to run the best race you can and finish.

His friend Cara added:

Live life like a marathon, not a sprint.

Richard Feynman was a theoretical physicist who won a Nobel prize. He was also a First Generation student, the son of struggling immigrants. He believed learning was simply about the thing itself. What does that mean? It isn't just about your grade or what someone else thinks of you or how you will use the knowledge. Success, he thought, is about getting your brain around understanding what it is you are learning. It's the joy of just knowing. That joy increases the odds of you finding your best path.

When things don't make sense, when everyone else seems to have an invisible rule book that you have never seen (See the section on *Unwritten Rules* in **Yes, You do Belong**, Chapter 4), standing curious rather than intimidated is a measure of success. Think about intimidation. Lots of students talk about being intimidated by teachers, or other students. The funny thing is that someone else has no ability to make you feel intimidated. You have to do it to yourself. You give yourself permission to feel intimidation. What if you adopted Farrah's philosophy and decided to feel curious instead?

Every time you figure out more about yourself, about how you learn best, when your internal clock allows you to study best, where you can find people who support and understand you, you are finding success. Jeep, disappointed with his early grades, figured out, "*I suck at listening and need movement, physical activity to learn. Now I record my notes and review them while walking around or running.*" Renu was paralyzed by anxiety attacks until her residential advisor walked her over to the campus therapy office. "*I have anxiety and depression. It was in therapy that I learned coping mechanisms and finally decided I'd benefit from medication. I now think that everyone who exists in this world should have a chance to see a therapist.*"

When you are scared to talk with a professor and you do, and it opens the door to a helpful relationship, that's success. When you want to give up on doing something you know you should do but it feels hard—and still, you do it, ring the success bell again. "*The first time I went to see a professor, my knees knocked. But I emerged alive and then it was never so hard again.*"

There is no greater measure of success than becoming aware of yourself—what you like, what you do well, what your gifts are, what excites you. Figuring out what you value and what you want to prioritize in life, that's success. Money, nice as it is, doesn't guarantee people the ability or focus to do this. There are men and women who drive big cars or eat in expensive restaurants, but you see they are jerks. Okay, laugh at this if you want, but in this book not being a jerk counts hands down as one measure of success.

A much-quoted Danish philosopher named Kierkegaard, who didn't find fame until long after his death, wrote that "**life can only be understood backwards, but it has to be lived forwards."** Kierkegaard called this "the dizziness of freedom." In the moment, we may be unsure how our actions will look to us in the future. But it helps to know that usually our decisions matter in some way. Another measure of success is working to make decisions consciously, rather than drifting because it feels easier. Trevor grew up as an only boy and the youngest in a family of strong-minded women.

> I had to do whatever the girls in the family decided to do. I so much wanted my voice to be heard that I acted out in school all the time and kept getting kicked out. It took me a long time to find myself. I dropped out of my first all-Black college. It was all men, all Baptist, all rules. Didn't last a semester at community college and failed out of the local state college. I failed the physical to go into the military. Once I slowed down and began to think about the consequences of my actions, when I saw my friends building stable lives and I had nothing, I knew I had to go back to school. Tell people they have to understand what they are doing and why they are doing it and what it is going to mean in the future.

"What one fool can understand, another can," wrote Richard Feynman, that Nobel prize winning physicist. The brain, your capacity to understand, is not determined by what clothes you are wearing, how much you spend on lunch, or what your parents do. It isn't even the result of where you went to high school, although high schools that provide a more rigorous preparation can reduce the time it takes to understand what some other fool seems to get quickly. **That you got yourself to college is already a measure of success.**

TAKE ACTION

Take a minute and write down how you have been measuring success until now. Do you want to set up new measures?

Pick a period of time—a month, a quarter, a year . . . and decide how, when the time has passed, you will judge success—but don't forget that learning from failure really is one measure of success.

3

EVERYBODY'S # 1 PIECE OF ADVICE

ASK!

If there is one overriding message that everyone wants you to hear, it can be summed up in one word: **ASK**.

As one young woman said, "*. . . and if you think you don't know the right question, well then ask somebody what the question should be.*" **Ask** for help with classes if you are struggling. **Ask** for help with your mental health if you are cratering. **Ask** for help with making difficult decisions if you are paralyzed. One young man went beyond **ask**. He likes the word, *demand*.

Why then is it so hard for students to ask for help? Dena says she was used to being a top student and didn't think she needed help:

> I thought that if I asked for help, it would mean I wasn't doing it on my own. I never wanted to admit I might be failing because I knew there was no safety net. I was carrying the vision for my whole family, and I didn't even want to admit to not doing well—even when I wasn't doing well.

When Isella went from a high school class of 83 to a university with over 8,000 freshmen, it felt overwhelming:

> There were many times when I was confused and didn't know what questions to ask. I didn't want to seem stupid, so I had to research a lot of stuff for myself. When I got to campus, I really didn't understand financial aid or how the money would appear. I learned early to just keep asking, and both the administrators and friends were really helpful.

Cecilia suggests one reason students are reluctant to look for outside resources:

> Maybe you grew up thinking it was wrong to ask for help, to let someone know what was going on with you. In immigrant families, it's a pride thing. You always have to show a good face. You came here for a better life, and you don't want anyone back home to know if you aren't doing well. Then you get more stressed, and it's a recurring pattern, and it is very stressful.

One incoming freshman read these paragraphs, and he did **ask**. He asked:

> Ask who?
> When should I ask?
> How do I ask?

He was quite serious. We were telling him how important asking is, and he said it felt like we were telling him to go play soccer without a playbook.

TAKE ACTION

How does the idea of asking others for help feel for you? Has there been a time(s) when you asked for help and were rewarded for the effort?

ASK WHO?

There are dozens of people you have available to you:

1. Advisors
2. Professors
3. Teaching Assistants
4. Counselors
5. Upper Classmen
6. People in your dorm
7. Program staff for multi-cultural, First Gen and/or minority students
8. Therapists
9. Employers
10. Mentors
11. Valued high school teachers or counselors
12. Study group peers
13. Financial Aid Office
14. Writing Center
15. Tutors
16. Librarians
17. Internet
18. Alums
19. Friends
20. Registrar

Part of the job of many on this list is to help students. You, the student, are central to the college's existence. You are supposed to **ask**, and faculty and staff are supposed to help you with answers. You have to do your job and allow them to do theirs.

Tai, thinking back to his painful family life, articulates just that point:

> There are people in the university who want you to succeed and want to help you. I never believed when I came to college that if the people who are supposed to care about me and help me, don't—well . . . why would some weird faculty stranger want me to succeed? Now I know that there are so many people who want to help you, way more than those who want to hurt you.

Ask different people the same question and compare answers. Make friends with someone in the offices—financial aid, the writing center, the library, etc.—where you are likely to need ongoing advice. It helps if someone knows your name, and you, theirs. (Look at the section on the *Value of Networking* in **Yes, You Do Belong,** Chapter 4.)

ASK WHEN?

Of course, see what you can figure out on your own. But don't get stuck going around in circles in your head telling yourself that if you were a better, different, smarter . . . whatever . . . person, you would understand. Usually, we have trouble understanding because we don't have enough information, or we are misinterpreting the information we have. So, go get more/better/clearer information.

You should ask whenever you don't know and find yourself unable to figure the answer out for yourself. Just so you know, here is a list of common situations that ought to move you to **ASK**:

- You have no idea what the professor is talking about in class.
- The material is difficult, and you don't have enough background to get a handle on it.
- You have tried to figure out how to do an assignment and remain confused.
- You are unclear about how your financial aid works, and it worries you.
- You think you might be entitled to more aid.
- You really need money and don't know where or how to find the right part-time job.
- You are getting grades that distress you and may threaten your scholarships.
- You feel lonely a lot of the time.
- You want to hide out and avoid people.
- You cry more than you believe is normal, or you feel rage.
- You don't know how to pick your courses or why you are in the ones you are in.

- You are considering dropping out.
- You are excited about things you are learning and want to talk with somebody about it.
- You would like a better living situation.
- You have food insufficiency.
- Your grades are okay, but you want to do better and are not sure how.
- You have unusual circumstances and wonder if there is a way to make things work around them.

There is a direct connection between your emotional state and your academic success. It is normal to feel overwhelmed by your college workload, by choosing a major, by dating, by talking with professors or even classmates. Don't be fooled by those who have an easy manner and seem to be sailing through. Yes, some students do. But not nearly as many as you are thinking have got it all together. *"Far more important than your GPA is your emotional health,"* Tanya counsels. *"Sure, college is meant to be a learning experience, a time of self-discovery, but it is not supposed to grind you down and make you feel like you never want to get out of bed."*

Having the courage to reach out and find a support system to help with whatever is weighing on you can take you from bleak to better.

ASK HOW?

How about this?

"First," Dre says, *"Smile."*

Introduce yourself and state your problem: *"Hi, I'm Dre Smith. I'm a freshman here and I'm hoping you could help me get unconfused about . . ."*

Maybe then you can briefly elaborate on the situation.

Again, **ask** for help: *"I would really value some help around this. I tried to figure it out myself, but I'm not getting anywhere."*

You can ask in person, on the phone, or by email. If you **ask** and don't get a response, **ask** again.

By the time you get around to asking for help, you might be angry. It's okay to feel angry, but it isn't usually effective to start a conversation in anger. Or maybe you are shy or hesitant. Sophia recommends, *". . . have a practice conversation with a friend or with the bathroom mirror."*

She also suggests: *"Bring a pencil and paper in case you want to write down things you learn so you don't forget."* Or ask to record the instructions on your phone.

Faculty office hours mean the door is open and you are free to come by, but sometimes it helps to use email to schedule an appointment with a person you need to see. If you have more than one question, make a list before you go and use it when you are there.

If you have gotten really good help, it's nice to follow up with a note of thanks by email or on paper.

If you ask and get an unhelpful answer, hold firm. Don't give up until you understand. You might have to ask again or find another person to ask, but understanding is the goal, so keep at it until you get what you need.

But there is another side to asking. A Black woman who went to a small eastern liberal arts college read what has been written here about asking, and said, *"It's fine to ask, but many people you ask have no understanding of the experiences of your life, so, yes—ask, but also tell."* When you are told things that don't make sense in the context of your life and feel wrong for you, let your voice be heard.

TAKE ACTION

Are there things that have been troubling you that you have hesitated to discuss? Think for a minute if you have been avoiding asking for information or help.

If that's the case, jot down the one or two most important to you and write down ideas about where you could get help and how and when you plan to ask.

You might also think about what you would like to 'tell' so that you feel seen and heard.

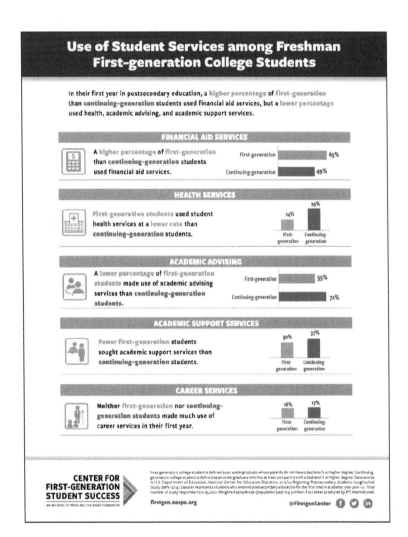

Use of Student Services among Freshman First-generation College Students

In their first year in postsecondary education, a higher percentage of first-generation than continuing-generation students used financial aid services, but a lower percentage used health, academic advising, and academic support services.

FINANCIAL AID SERVICES

A higher percentage of first-generation than continuing-generation students used financial aid services.

First-generation 65%
Continuing-generation 49%

HEALTH SERVICES

First-generation students used student health services at a lower rate than continuing-generation students.

First-generation 14%
Continuing-generation 29%

ACADEMIC ADVISING

A lower percentage of first-generation students made use of academic advising services than continuing-generation students.

First-generation 55%
Continuing-generation 72%

ACADEMIC SUPPORT SERVICES

Fewer first-generation students sought academic support services than continuing-generation students.

First-generation 30%
Continuing-generation 37%

CAREER SERVICES

Neither first-generation nor continuing-generation students made much use of career services in their first year.

First-generation 16%
Continuing-generation 17%

CENTER FOR FIRST-GENERATION STUDENT SUCCESS
AN INITIATIVE OF NASPA AND THE SUDER FOUNDATION

firstgen.naspa.org   @FirstgenCenter

First-generation college student is defined as an undergraduate whose parents do not have a bachelor's or higher degree. Continuing-generation college student is defined as an undergraduate who has at least one parent with a bachelor's or higher degree. Data source is U.S. Department of Education, National Center for Education Statistics, 2012/14 Beginning Postsecondary Students Longitudinal Study (BPS 12/14). Dataset represents students who entered postsecondary education for the first time in academic year 2011–12. Total number of study respondents is 25,000. Weighted sample size (population size) is 4.3 million. Fact sheet produced by RTI International.

4

YES,
YOU DO BELONG

MINOR SETBACK.
MAJOR COMEBACK

Gerrie, Yvonne, and Tai all came to college with good academic records and a hunger to learn. What made each of them, and so many others, initially feel knocked off balance? As they tell their stories, it is the sudden and acute intersection of people from different social classes.

That pretty much sums up the way many First Gen students, the majority of whom have family incomes below the national median, describe their initial immersion into college environments. An immediate and personal cultural clash makes them wonder, initially, *Do I really belong here?*

Interviewees talked about fish-out-of-water feelings. A high schooler from Texas had a chance to spend the summer at an elite private school in Maine. *"This was the first time I found myself in an all-Caucasian world. I felt really uncomfortable, like my brown skin stood out everywhere."* A young man whose family sacrificed for him to go to Catholic school was shocked to find his roommate didn't believe in God. A Yalie from Texas recalls too vividly his own fish-out-of-water pains in the presence of affluent and seemingly condescending parents of friends. Tai describes his hands trembling when he realized all the other Asians he is meeting come from families much more affluent than his. A young woman from a small western town still remembers the shock of a roommate with a $2000 coat. A mentor is stunned to discover her mentee carried the weight of her mother's addiction and mental illness as a heavy secret from the world for all four years of college to avoid perceived social class prejudices.

Sophia grew up in Houston, the daughter of parents who immigrated from Mexico in the eighties. She was surprised by her discomfort when she arrived at the state's flagship university in Austin.

> Some of the stuff my classmates talked about, I didn't know anything about. I didn't know many of the American cultural touchstones like the Backstreet Boys. I didn't know if it was okay to speak Spanish, and I always had this scenario in my head about what I would say if I was told to speak English.

What is social class? Commonly it is defined by three things:

1. Financial capital, which is about money and resources available due to financial influence.
2. Social capital, which is about how connected we are to other people in the world and our ability to use our networks to reach our goals.
3. Cultural capital, which is measured by what we know and what we do in the world.

(If you want to know more about social class, an article in this footnote is a place to start.[3])

Now, sometimes people also speak about emotional capital, our ability to manage the highs and lows of life; and also, spiritual capital, which has less defined clarity but addresses our comfort with spiritual values.[4]

---

3   https://news.gallup.com/opinion/polling-matters/204497/determines-americans-perceive-social-class.aspx
4   https://metanexus.net/what-spiritual-capital-economics-religion-and-conference-2006/

When Gallup, the polling organization, asks people to describe their social class they use five categories: upper, upper-middle, middle, working, and lower. Generally, there is correlation between class, income, and education. If you grew up hanging out with people who saw themselves in one class and you are suddenly plunged into another class, one with different financial and social capital, it can be uncomfortable.

More than one First Gen talked about finding classmates who not only had better clothes and much more disposable income for beer and pizza, but also had experiences that were "*disorienting.*" One recalls discussions about skiing and sailing and family trips that "*blew my mind.*"

"*If your dad is a janitor or you never had a dad, it can feel humbling to hear of parents, both moms and dads, who are doctors, lawyers and wealthy businesspeople. It is easy to feel that peers will look down on you if they know your dad is a janitor.*" Students who had to work to have any money found themselves resenting their peers who had only to study. (See Chapter 7 on **Money**)

The American credo is that we live in a fluid society. We judge people on merit, not money or job titles. But, of course, that isn't exactly what happens. If you find yourself in an environment where you feel odd-man-out, where your peers have had the chance to learn intellectual, social and emotional information that is new to you, it can knock you off-balance for a while. It's what made Lee want to pretend she fit in to her college life when she definitely felt the opposite. It's what made Val angry and Jeep determined to crack the code.

One reason it feels important to address social class head-on is to underscore the difference between events that are in your control and those that are happening around you, but not because of you. Some things that happen are the results of our own actions. If you don't start the term paper with enough time to do good work, your professor may have harsh comments. That's on you. But some of what happens are offshoots of what is happening culturally. Your thoughtful comments at the seminar table are ignored because there are cultural myths about whose voice is valuable. You interview for a job, and it goes to someone you know is less qualified. The point is to be aware of what you can fix and what may take more than just you to fix it. Do not hold yourself responsible for actions that are buried in a culture that has misplaced ideas about power and status. **Institutions have built-in biases that are invisible to those not hurt by them.**

It may help a bit to think about how we all have bits of prejudice inside of us. Harold Bloom, renowned teacher, writer and critic, thought that "human beings can hardly get through the day without prejudices of all sorts—ingrained beliefs about the way things are, or ought to be, that go largely unexamined."[5] Bloom thought some prejudices may actually be good for us because they give us constraining social norms and supportive values that we shouldn't give up. But there is a difference between *believing* something is good for us and *deciding* that what's good for us should be good for everybody or that what's normal for us is really what normal should be for all.

Knowing we have our own prejudices—and looking at them close up—is part of our education. Bravo. Maybe it helps just a bit to see that we are led to believe things because of the way we grew

---

5   https://www.thepublicdiscourse.com/2019/08/56257/

up and that if we can change, so can others. That recognized, let's move on to the uncomfortable truth that almost every student with whom we talked felt the pressures of class difference. In the face of disagreeable prejudice, whether recognized or not by the person who holds it, or more subtle class discrimination, Harold Bloom's theories are not so comforting. Maybe we have to end with the student who conveys his blunt message, *Don't let that shit get to you.* Or maybe you want to end with the voice of the graduate who says, *Don't tolerate anything that demeans you.*

TAKE ACTION

Are there things about college that have surprised you?
Are there things about yourself that have surprised you?

QUOTES FROM STUDENTS WHO ALL WENT ON TO DO JUST FINE IN COLLEGE

"That first year, I was completely scared. I wanted to quit. I was one of the smartest kids in high school, but how was I going to compete with all of these super-smart kids in college? I was sure I couldn't do it."

"In the beginning, college was surreal."

"It was a nightmare at the start. I had some college in Albania, but I didn't understand anything. I had no idea what an essay was or how to understand math. I lived at the tutoring center."

"I knew I was going to fail. It was only when my learning center forced me to get tutors and use faculty office hours that I understood there were resources to help me. The real turning point, however, was when I became part of the campus TRIO program."

"It is an out-of-body experience when everything you see is completely contrary to what you grew up with, and you don't feel like you are really there, but you are."

"I always loved Spanish and wanted to excel in my Spanish class, but everyone was better than me. They had stories of living abroad or traveling, and I felt like I wasn't good enough."

"When I went into Philadelphia, I felt like I was the only Hispanic and everyone was looking at me. I definitely had the imposter syndrome."

"There were times when I was so confused. I didn't even know what questions to ask."

"My first day, I kept thinking "Who am I?" It took me a year to get comfortable."

"In the beginning, I was paralyzed. I kept asking myself, "How am I going to be as good as my peers who have all the money and help in the world?"

"I walked on that big, diverse campus and had culture shock. I didn't know how to make connections and was afraid others wouldn't understand my circumstances."

WHAT HELPED?

AND THESE ARE THINGS STUDENTS SAY HELPED THEM GET COMFORTABLE

"Finding a mentor made all the difference."

"It was my job at the gym that helped me meet people and feel like I belonged there."

"Being in a theme house gave me a safe space where I felt understood."

"Remembering that I am paving the way for others gave me purpose."

"Joining a campus program for First Generation students changed everything."

"Deciding I could take a chance and join some campus organizations made all the difference."

"Hanging out with people like me helped me feel comfortable."

"The summer orientation program meant I started college knowing both peers and faculty, so I didn't feel so strange."

"Asking for help made all the difference"

"I had to get over wanting to hide the fact that I was a First Generation student from a poor family."

"I just kept telling myself it was an amazing thing that I could go to college and could be on this campus, and nobody could take that away from me."

"I knew that I had been successful in the past and so I could figure out how to be successful there."

IGNORE THE
IMPOSTER SYNDROME

There are about 20 million students enrolled in U.S. colleges right now. Surely, they cannot all be smarter, more deserving and harder working than you.

So many interviewees had moments when they felt they didn't really belong in their colleges, and any minute, someone would tap them on the shoulder and say, sorry, it was all a mistake.

That's not truth. It's the imposter syndrome. Seventy percent of all people have at least one bout of imposter syndrome in their lives—and that includes professors.

Imposters suffer from chronic self-doubt and a sense of intellectual fraudulence that override any feelings of success or external proof of their competence. They seem unable to internalize their accomplishments, no matter how successful they are in their field. High achieving, highly successful people often suffer, so imposter syndrome doesn't equate with low self-esteem or a lack of self-confidence. In fact, some researchers have linked it with perfectionism, especially in women and among academics.[6]

6 https://www.verywellmind.com/imposter-syndrome-and-social-anxiety-disorder-4156469
   There are several very good TED talks on the internet. Hunt around. Maybe start with this:
   https://www.youtube.com/watch?v=GT_1xv2dk10

"I had no anxieties about going to college," Fernando tells us, looking back at his freshman year at an Ivy League school:

 I had spent a summer in India and one at an exclusive D.C. prep school studying politics. I didn't worry.

I got to college three days early for a pre-orientation for minority and disadvantaged students. There were about 100 of us and it was great. I was happy. Then on day four, everyone else arrived. That night we met in our small freshman groups of a dozen students and a graduate advisor, And, wham, it hit me. These people were nothing like me. I was the only non-Caucasian in the room. I had this unspoken but inbred association about racial differences and the power and status of Caucasians. I didn't speak a word in class for my first two years of college. I kept thinking 'How am I going to be as good as these kids around me who had all this money and help in the world?'

But you don't have to go to an Ivy League school to feel like an imposter. Malcolm went from upstate New York to an all-Black men's college in the South. *"I hadn't grown up where Blackness was everywhere, and I worried that I wasn't Black enough like students who had gone to this college for generations."* Jeep went to a top state university while still on probation for a misdemeanor.

 I was used to talking to people who had dropped out of high school. I didn't understand how to talk to people on that campus. I felt very uncomfortable and went into a shell. What helped was meeting someone who, like me, loved basketball, and he got me into a fraternity and those guys helped me understand all the unwritten rules.

(See section below on *Unwritten Rules.*)

Feeling like an imposter can make you want to hide. Fernando was not the only student never to say a word in any class the entire freshman year—sometimes longer—for fear everyone would think he was stupid. Of course, one senior said he later realized that almost everyone sounds sort of stupid, which is why you are in college. Cecilia recalls never speaking up to faculty *"because I was sure I wasn't what they wanted."* Caucasian students like Stacy struggle with whether to pretend they just fit in or be honest about their fears and challenges. *"I noticed that people don't assume all people of color are First Generation students, but they assume all First Generation students are people of color."* In reality, more than 40% of First Generation students are White.

Some students of color think they are seen as having gotten to college because of special privilege and that their classmates feel they don't really belong or have unfairly taken someone's place who is more worthy. In fact, schools are richer and better equipped to educate when students are diverse, and all kinds of voices and experiences are represented in the classroom. There are enough chairs in this country for everyone to get an education. Make the best of the chair you have.

Feeling you don't really belong can trigger an oddly-named syndrome, John Henryism: trying to overcome chronic stress by working harder and harder.[7] John Henryism can make you sick. Of course, you do need to work hard, but balance will help you work successfully. *"Do not spend all your time in the dorm studying like my unhappy friend,"* Mai tells you. *"Join clubs, talk*

---

7   https://unhealthywork.org/psychological-risk-factors/john-henryism-and-cardiovascular-health/ Also see https://academic.oup.com/aje/article-abstract/126/4/664/166269?redirected From=PDF

to people those first weeks on campus before you have papers and midterms. Upper classmen know how hard it is and are super-friendly. You will meet the people who can help you with all sorts of stuff and will become your study-buddies. Studying with others helps so much, but you have to have the courage to leave the dorm and go looking for organizations in those early weeks when they are all looking for you.

TAKE ACTION

Have you experienced the imposter syndrome? Would it be useful to have an anti-imposter syndrome mantra you can recite to yourself when your brain tries to suggest you are not as capable as you really are?

What of value are you bringing to your campus?

RACE

Social class is not the same as race, but class and race issues get mixed up. And since more than half of First Generation college students are people of color, race issues were a low hum in the background of many interviews and seemed important to discuss. It felt difficult to know what to write, but then, in the middle of editing this chapter, George Floyd, an unarmed Black man in Minneapolis, was murdered by police. Black Lives Matter protests exploded across the United States. Race became a topic that demanded conversation and, at the same time, made conversation ever more complicated. Was it right, I wondered; was it possible for me as a White woman of privilege to be able to write with relevance?

It was obvious that I could not possibly summarize feelings around this or begin to unravel the illogic that claims to order people by race. What this book can do is present the voices of others, most of whom were interviewed before the entire nation rightfully focused so intently on race. In offering comments from interviewees, I invite you to run the comments through your own filters.

This section is not only for people of color. Race is an issue for all of us, and all of us have a responsibility to help eradicate behaviors that demean, limit, and hurt humankind because of skin color or religious beliefs. If being White, no matter our social class, infers privileges, it also infers responsibilities.[8]

---

8   Watch https://www.youtube.com/watch?v=ebPoSMULI5U. This 30 min Oprah show provides
    a powerful example of how racism is a learned irrational behavior.

"Race was always an issue," Val says.

> My family is from El Salvador but kids at prep school called me the Mexican. They never bothered to learn how to pronounce my full name correctly. At college the microaggressions were more veiled but still there. And I never said anything because I didn't want to be labeled a hypersensitive liberal who couldn't take it. At college, I still didn't speak up because part of me told myself I was just freeloading there, and I should just take it and be grateful. It took me a long time to tell myself I had earned my place there.

Stanley thought he might join a fraternity. When invitations to mixers came out, all the guys on his corridor got at least one invitation—except him. *"It wasn't personality since it was too early for anyone to know people. I was just invisible."*

Cara was sure she was the opposite of invisible. *"When I left campus to go into the city, I felt like I was the only person there with brown skin and it flashed like a neon light."* Stan used to count the number of minorities in every class and hate it when he was the only one. *"This is the reason,"* Roberto insists, *"why community college was such a great way to start for me. You need a place where you can feel safe and welcomed and build a network of people who understand just what you are facing."*

Many interviewees say that finding people who understand your cultural circumstances and have shared your experiences can mean so much. Melanie left home for a large flagship university. Her comfort was living in a theme house, a floor of a dorm, especially for the Latinx communities. (Five other theme houses at her school orient to other communities.) *"In lots of my classes, I was the only Chicana. It is comforting to come back to my room and find people who have experiences similar to mine. It can be intimidating to stand out and to feel people don't value our real-world experiences."*

Ife says she didn't feel overt race issues on campus but was so aware of how few people of color were in any room.

> I spent most of my time in the co-op where I lived and didn't hang out much on campus at first. But then I got bored. I realize how being scared just puts you in a corner. When I decided to connect, I got involved in a satirical publication on campus, but what has been so great is joining a writing room for comedy. Comedy makes you so vulnerable and it made me more comfortable in speaking out.

Yvonne came from a poor immigrant family and never expected to end up at the University of California's San Diego campus, the first in her family ever to live away from Los Angeles, away from her neighborhood of poverty and crime.

> I certainly had social anxiety at college—except I didn't know what that was. I think I was depressed for the first six months. I was afraid other people wouldn't understand my circumstances, and I didn't know how to make connections. And when others made me feel uncomfortable, when things hurt, I would just remember why I was there. That I ended up standing on that campus was such an accomplishment, and I always wanted to embrace that . . . I would tell others to think about how they are paving the way. This is what I was doing, and I kept that in the front of my mind.

An aerospace engineering major, now in his sophomore year at a big California university, articulated his feelings as an African American:

> Being Black, you don't see that many familiar faces. It's like imagining how an alien would feel on Earth, hard to connect or talk because you have nothing in common. You feel you are living in different worlds. Being a minority, being Black, it's its own struggle. It can beat you down or build you up. I just pick and choose my battles and don't give up.

Joining the campus chapter of Black engineers is one decision that he found helpful and recommends looking for race-based professional groups.

Other students embraced activism. Dre formed a First Gen group on campus with the explicit intention of showing the strengths those students were bringing to his large Midwest campus. Malcolm ended up walking away from a career in finance, where he felt racial prejudice worked against him, to get a degree in education and teach about race. He connected me with an American University panel discussion he had moderated on Educational Equity and Justice. Students there said, *"When you are an 'only', embrace it."* Panelists urged teachers, their fellow students and themselves to speak up and make visible the microaggressions that so often pass unmarked. *"Your silence may be someone else's violence,"* Malcolm told the audience. But Black faculty members caution students who become active to practice self-care. Activism itself can be both healing and emotionally roiling.

Microaggressions are the everyday verbal, nonverbal, and environmental slights, snubs, or insults, whether intentional or unintentional, that communicate hostile, derogatory, or negative messages to target persons based solely upon their marginalized group membership.[9]

The term was coined by psychiatrist and Harvard University professor, Chester M. Pierce, to describe insults and dismissals which he regularly witnessed non-Black Americans inflicting on African Americans. Now it is applied beyond the Black community.

Both interviewees and discussions in the literature discuss different kinds of responses. Where there seems to be widespread agreement is that when you experience microaggressions, it can be helpful and even necessary to discuss your cognitive and emotional reactions with people who care about you, or with mental health professionals, to avoid accumulating negative and detrimental feelings which can affect your emotional well-being. It shouldn't be your responsibility to create a campus environment which allows you to be safe from trauma, but if wishes had wings, sheep would fly. See the section on *Depression and Anxiety* in Chapter 6, **The Importance of Emotional Well Being**, for a further discussion on the effects of racism.

One student posted an online note urging students to read Paulio Freire's *Pedagogy of the Oppressed*. Another thought that reading Lisa Depit's work on the *culture of power* provided a helpful context for understanding those fish-out-of-water feelings. The

9   https://academicaffairs.ucsc.edu/events/documents/Microaggressions_Examples_Arial_
    2014_11_12.pdf; https://advancingjustice-la.org/sites/default/files/ELAMICRO%20A_Guide_
    to_Responding_to_Microaggressions.pdf

Internet now is full of suggested readings for those who struggle with what racism is.

What can be said about the stupidity of discrimination, intentional and unintentional? You can't fix it alone. You might think about whether First Gens on campus, as a group, could be instrumental in helping their institutions; as one student put it, "... *to go beyond tolerating diversity to embracing diversity.*"

TAKE ACTION

When you hear microaggressions directed at others, how might you respond?

If you have experienced microaggressions, are you satisfied with your responses or could you consider other ways of handling it?

THE UNWRITTEN RULES

Jeep said in an earlier comment that he needed help learning the *"unwritten rules."* What are they?

They are unwritten because they only exist in people's minds. They are assumptions about how we do things around here, and those who follow them get rewarded and those who don't, get penalized for ignoring rules they didn't know existed. You can't really look them up in the library. This is watch-and-learn stuff, but mentors, advisors and friends can all help.

"I didn't know anything. I didn't know what college was. I didn't know what I was supposed to be doing. I just knew survival. I made mistakes," remembers the daughter of Hmong refugees, now finishing a Ph.D., *"but I don't make those mistakes anymore."*

The unwritten rules you encounter at college are expectations about behavior that come from the dominant culture and are assumed to be logical and generally understood without discussion. You may be the intellectual equal of your classmates. You may have the same skin color, the same drive and curiosity, but if they are operating by a set of unwritten rules that you don't know exist, it can certainly feel like you are playing on an uneven field.

In college, these may show up as not understanding that faculty office hours mean students are welcome to come to the instructor's office or that tutoring is a good thing, and not a mark of inadequacy. These misunderstandings keep First Generation students from feeling comfortable joining campus groups or study sessions, but they also inhibit traditional students from interacting with those who seem different and bring fresh perspectives.

We cannot know what we have never been taught or exposed to. There is no inadequacy in not knowing some of the academic or social stuff that more affluent kids take for granted. It is not hard to learn, and you will learn it, if you find it is useful for you. It is harder for affluent kids to learn what it means to grapple with poverty. They seldom feel inadequate for not knowing the nuances of your life, so don't let yourself feel inadequate for not knowing the nuances of theirs.

Presentation and appearance are governed by unwritten rules. One young woman wrote about how her roommates called her *"ghetto"* for the way she talked. Several said they had become adept at *"code switching."* Lee explained that she learned to talk one way at college, but when she went home to her small rural town in Iowa, she switched back to a local speech pattern. *"People make judgments about your intellectual capabilities based on how well you use conventional grammar. If you didn't grow up speaking a certain way and if your high school teachers sometimes used the same linguistic forms, how are you supposed to know there is another way to talk that people assume is better?"* Jerrie says she uses *". . . college talk in my high-tech company, but I need ghetto talk with my family."*

Here are some other *unwritten rules* moments that surprised students:

"I was always a good student, so I had no idea what the difference between my papers and others was until we had a group exercise that required we critique our classmates' essays. Only then did I understand there were standards I hadn't grasped."

"My roommate invited me home for a weekend. His family was great. I had no idea I was supposed to write a thank you note afterwards."

"Going to a dinner seminar traumatized me. I suddenly felt like I didn't know how to eat."

"I was invited to a birthday party for a friend. I was surprised we were all expected to chip in for a gift."

"It was a surprise to show up at a campus event and find I was the only guy in shorts and a tee shirt."

"It stunned me to find out that half the people on my corridor had lined up summer jobs through family connections."

In the **ASK** chapter, we talked about students being told to ask, but not understanding who to ask or when or how. If in your family, the unspoken rule is that asking for help equates weakness, how are you supposed to know that at college, it is considered a sign of strength? If you feel unseen or misunderstood by faculty and peers but cautioned by your family not to stand out, what does it take to see the value of interacting?

In rooms where others, consciously or unconsciously make you feel invisible, when do you decide you will benefit from visibility? Can you embrace how impressive an accomplishment it is that you are in college and that you are earning a place that may allow you to influence the rules?

The importance of having social capital to use and the role networking plays in accumulating that social capital is often very clear to traditional students, but not to First Gens, so we are including a section below specifically addressing that unwritten rule.

TAKE ACTION

Does your family have unwritten rules? Are there some you want to cherish? Are there some you want to re-consider?

Do you already have a sense of unwritten rules on your campus?

NETWORKING ADDS
TO YOUR NET WORTH

Certainly, you want friends who look like you and understand your family history, who like the food your mother makes and appreciate the nuances of your cultural background. But you also benefit from friends who just share your interests and stimulate your thinking and may not look like you.

The friends you make in college can become a valued support network after you graduate. The more diverse that network, the more help you can have navigating the world later. Contacts matter. They matter for all of us, and if your family lacks a helpful network, for sure, friends matter.

One Latino man who graduated a few years ago from a big-name university told us he had several First Gen friends from the same school who were now unemployed or underemployed. *"We all did fine at school, but we had no idea how to leverage our education when we finished. We did not take it for granted that we were going to fit into the predominantly Caucasian world and had no role models to reassure us."* He goes on to explain that several of his peers are lost in figuring out how to navigate the work world because there was no class in networking, no appreciation for how the world worked after college, and no parents to help.

One of the major reasons that networking is an effective way to get a job is that there is something of a hidden job market out there. Some estimate that as much as 80 percent of new jobs are never listed but are instead filled internally or via networking.

A referral from someone who is already working with a company is a big advantage. Only seven percent of job applicants get this kind of referral, yet referrals make up 40 percent of new hires. Clearly, networking isn't just one potential route to finding a new job—it's actually the most effective path.

"At least 70 percent, if not 80 percent, of jobs are not published," the president of Career Horizons told NPR.

> And yet most people—they are spending 70 or 80 percent of their time surfing the net versus getting out there, talking to employers, taking some chances [and] realizing that the vast majority of hiring is friends and acquaintances hiring other trusted friends and acquaintances.[10]

This is not an invitation to be manipulative and only interested in people who can potentially be useful. It is, again, encouragement for you to make friends widely across all kinds of groups. Your friends and their friends and their parents and their parents' friends can all be these contacts referred to above. But a person has to know you, like you and appreciate your strengths in order to help you find a job. **They can't know you if you never talk to them, if you fail to interact and let your real self be seen.**

A good network doesn't only help with jobs. It can help you find the right living situation, the best pizza in town, a person to date, good books to read, and where to get your glasses repaired. Being part of a community means you don't have to figure everything out for yourself. Your friends will know things you don't, and you will be able to share information they need.

---

10 https://www.payscale.com/career-news/2017/04/many-jobs-found-networking

"More people want to help you than you imagine." It is not an imposition to ask someone for help. Most people feel good about helping someone else. If people don't want to help you, they won't. Unless you ask, you'll never know. Remember, employers are looking to hire people who come well recommended, who have been vetted by someone known to them. Being recommended doesn't mean you get the job. You have to get the job yourself, but contacts can create the opportunity for you to close the deal.

Cecelia finally decided to apply for a graduate counseling program, but she had missed the deadline. Her professor made a call, and she was in. Jorge's prior felony was going to keep him from campus housing. His mentor wrote some letters, and he got the house. Prisha was having trouble with tuition, but from her campus work, she knew lots of people in administration. Her scholarship was increased. A community contact put Fernando on to his current university job. Quentin still gets career advice from the men he worked with during a high school internship. Starr's mentor helped her pay off her debts. Not everyone gets lucky, but if you never engage outside your comfort zone, there is no chance you will either.

It is helpful to know other First Gen students who share your feelings and culture. Again and again, interviewees tell us how important it is to hang out with people who "get" you, with no explanation. *"Outside of class, most of my friends were minorities,"* says Farrah who was at a predominately White university. Theresa explains that, *"mingling with people of privilege doesn't give you privilege. In the face of microaggressions, it helps to be around people who can understand and with whom you can discuss it."*

But please don't exclude friendships with people because you think they grew up in a bubble of privilege. Don't hold that against them any more than you want your status to be held against you. Sara regrets that *"I only hung out with people of color. I didn't expose myself to White people, didn't realize until senior year that I could have things in common with White people."* One day your classmates are going to be graduates out in the working world. You may be able to help them, and they may be able to help you. It is a pleasure to help people we know and like, and it happens all the time.

Look for opportunities to get to know people who are further along than you. Maybe they are alums who mentor students on campus or faculty, staff, or teachers. Maybe they are parents of friends or people for whom you work. Find a program on your campus specifically designed to foster mentorships. Listen to the scores of voices telling you to do this. Develop a relationship with these adults. *"Use your school's alumni data base. If you don't want to use the phone, send an email. These people can help you connect if you have to move to a new city."*

If you have a chance to be connected with someone interested in mentoring, take it. You are going to need references, connections, and contacts from all parts of the community. A big part of privilege is having those connections, and if your family cannot provide them easily, create them for yourself. This is as much a part of your college work as classes. And don't forget to use your classes as a vehicle for developing relationships with faculty. A UCSD senior advises students to create reasons to use faculty hours. *"Find a real question or issue that you can use to initiate a conversation during faculty hours. You want your professors to know who you are, and assuming you deserve it, to think well of you, because you are likely going to need letters of reference down the line. Professors can't write a good letter if they don't know you."*

Friendships come most easily through shared activities—sports, study groups, campus organizations, volunteering, and jobs. *"Volunteering can help defeat feelings of isolation and uselessness. I felt those acutely when I moved to New York City for a summer with no network,"* Eduardo recalls. Several students writing essays for TRIO (a federal outreach program for under-served students) spoke about how volunteering with their colleges' TRIO program gave them a place on campus to call home. And if, like Nadia, you spend so much time working that it feels impossible to join study groups or clubs, use your work as an opportunity to network.

Prisha described how falling into running for the student union to do a favor for a friend changed her life by opening her to the possibilities of social action. She ended up being Student Body President, which was a paid job that later opened the door to deeply satisfying experiences and contacts.

Maybe you want to set a specific number of new people you are going to meet each semester that you feel you can call friends and, likewise, a specific number of adults that you feel know you and like you and you like them in return. These people are going to be part of your post-graduation support team. And maybe they are going to support you in summer work as well.

Annika now knows that being unaware of the need to develop work contacts related to her field while still in college hurt her after graduation:

> I always saw summer as just a time to make money. I went home and found a job nearby. I took the job that paid the most and gave me the longest hours. I was an industrial design major, but it never occurred to me to look for a job that would help me with my career. Some classmates could afford to do unpaid internships, but I had to earn all my own spending money, and I knew I couldn't manage with unpaid work. I didn't try to figure out how I might get work that paid and also related to my academic studies. It was short-sighted of me.

Annika says her family ". . . *assumed that when I graduated from college, I would go do something important and wonderful—and be well-paid.*" And because they believed it, she believed it too. She was surprised to find a more complicated work world than she had imagined.

Let your professors—and your friends—know what you want from them. Be specific. Ask for their help in a gracious and undemanding way. Most people don't actually provide much help—but it only takes one helping of help to get you where you need to be.

TAKE ACTION

On paper or in your head, list your strengths. Think about what you bring to campus that seems in short supply. Long time ago I heard a story about a parent writing a college admissions officer saying, "It is well-known that your school looks for leaders. My daughter has the ability to be a great follower. All those leaders need people like her."

Are there a few people you would like to know better? Make a plan for how you will connect with them.

5

FAMILY

PUSHES AND PULLS

It is a big-hearted story when parents or guardians with little education themselves, who barely speak English and struggle to pay the bills, insist their children get an education, do "better" in the world than they did and have less punishing work. Mothers move in search of better school districts. Fathers overcome a deep reluctance to let their daughters leave home. Parents sign loans they can ill-afford to make college possible. Grandparents find energy to parent when they thought that task was done. Their children tell these stories with pride and love. In a minute, we'll acknowledge the young people who have more painful experiences.

Quentin remembers that freshman year, he was so homesick and wanted to transfer home. *"My mom wouldn't let me. She told me I had to do something with my life."* Eduardo recounts how relentless his mother was in finding the best school programs for her children. Maria credits her mother for pushing her into the middle school program that let her see college as a possibility and figure out how to apply.

Eduardo, when asked if he felt a distance from his immigrant family now that he was a top-school graduate, said, *"No. I took care of that my first vacation home. I taught my family what I had learned. I taught them 'elite college jargon'. We have a family creed: We all advance together."*

For Mai, going to college did not distance her from her Vietnamese parents. *"College made me appreciate my parents more. I saw how much I just took for granted."*

Many times, interviewees explained that the belief, the drive, the faith of the people who cared for them is what led them to college and kept them there. But in some cases, families don't understand the desire for college; maybe they feel they are being abandoned or demeaned. They made it without college, therefore cannot see the value. Or the unrelenting demands of survival and daily grind of never having enough money to pay bills makes a child's desire to go to college seem frivolous, even selfish. Not having the support of our caretakers can undermine our self-confidence. *Am I selfish? Am I unloving? Am I foolish?* These questions echo in the minds of First Generation students whose families do not understand the desire for more education.

But sometimes, it cuts the other way. So much is expected of you, so many family hopes are riding on your success, that you doubt you can live up to them. There is enormous pressure to figure out a way to make money, do something important, bring honor to the family. Your family is sure they know the right occupation for you—and you find you are not so sure. What to think?

What you might think is that each of us is given one life here now. We have lots of responsibilities in that life, but none is more central than becoming the best person that we can be, growing into all our capacities. And no one, not even a parent who loves us beyond words, can feel what we feel or control us the way we can control ourselves. The work of growing up is to figure out who we are and how we want to be in the world. That's huge and takes energy and focus. It just takes time to figure out who we want to grow into and having that time is one of the gifts of college.

At the same time that you are growing and changing, you don't want to lose that connection with home that grounds you in who you are. Lee grew up in a small western town. Her mother, she says, had a clear vision for her that college was the way out, but had no idea how to coach her on applying.

> I only got to college because my best friend's mom was the town librarian and when she took her daughter for the college test, I just went along. I ended up being a national merit scholar and was accepted widely, but I was too terrified to go far. I went to the state university.
>
> There is a degree of loss and sacrifice that happens when you go off to college . . . By the time I went across country for graduate work, my family had no idea what I did or why I was doing it. And, in fact, I'm not sure I really understand their world since I only knew it as a child . . . Nobody talks about language, but if I don't code switch when I go home, if I still sound like a college professor, it makes people feel ashamed and that makes me an outsider. I love what I do, but sometimes I feel some regret.

A college graduate, now with a family of her own, struggles with wanting to disconnect from her family of origin:

> They are completely dysfunctional. They make awful choices. They only care about what I can do for them. My husband and I have real struggles, yet my family seems to think I am the one who has it made. It has been very difficult for me to come to the point where I stop letting them make me feel bad.

All stories are not sad. Many interviewees talked about how glad they are their parent would not let them quit, feel despair, or transfer home. They were grateful for parental support and proud that their parents believed they were role models for the family and community.

It's easier, Eduardo thinks, if your family has some context . . . if they know a little about the larger world. *"I see that my friends whose parents really don't understand an American way of life, who grew up in another culture and did not have a chance for education, really find it hard to comprehend college and all it brings."*

"I went to college and all my family and friends carried on as they were. At first, it felt like a barrier," Jeep says, *"and then I realized that the barrier was just an idea in my head. I decided there would not be a barrier. Now, when I go home, I try to do work with my parents or my siblings, and it gives us points of commonality."*

Being in college changes you. It is meant to do that. It may mean that opening the door to a larger world makes you feel claustrophobic in your old world. Be patient with your family and hope they can be patient with you.

FAMILY PRESSURES

Avoid adding to your struggles by bad family feelings. If you have parents who work hard and love you and you love them, be proud of them. Don't let other lifestyles let you see your parents for less than they are. If you have parents struggle because they have let addictions get in their way, don't forget that addiction is not limited to lower income people. It's just easier for more affluent people to hide it. Your parents' decisions are not about you. You have made it to college, and that is a shower of stars on your chart.

If you have parents you can't respect, this is a sadness. They may be suffering the consequences of inadequate parenting from their own parents. All you can do now is be a better parent when it is your turn. Don't waste valuable energy in fighting family. Focus on building the best life for you that you can and, if possible, help your siblings. Starr put herself through college after getting pregnant in high school and went on to build her own stable family and career; she has struggled with family feelings:

 We are barely making it with two kids and one of us in school and my father is calling and asking me for money. How crazy is that? My sisters are married to drug dealers, one of whom is in prison. My dad drinks. My mom spends her life babysitting her grandkids, who are growing up not speaking English. I want to save them all, and I struggle with that. But I finally got it that trying to save them means giving up what we are working toward, and then I probably can't succeed with them anyway. It hurts, it really hurts, to tell myself I have to let go . . . but I have to let go.

What do you do if your family is in crisis and asks for you to help with money? This is very hard. It is likely that in the long run, the best way to help your family is to earn your degree and use it to find good work that will earn you enough to help them as well as yourself. Short term—that's harder. You have to ask yourself if this seems like a one-time problem or is it part of a pattern that will happen again? As a young person, you should not be responsible for taking care of your family. It is not your job to heal your parents' wounds. The task you face is not to let those wounds leave you permanently wounded. But do you let them get evicted, do without heat, absent themselves from a loved one's passing? You know there is no easy answer. One possibility is to meet with the Dean of Students to ask if it is possible to arrange a no-interest loan to help your family so you can stay in school, graduate and pay it back. That won't always be an option, but it's worth exploring.

Is it really selfish to insist on building your own life, on putting the value of an education first? Or is it brave? Is it wise? Cecilia still feels some guilt that she refused to come home when her mother was struggling with mental health issues. *"My sister left college and stepped into my mom's role. I wouldn't come home. I just stayed away and pretended nothing was happening. Now I feel guilty and my family thinks I am selfish, but there was nothing I could do, and I didn't want to leave school."*

"My family, a graduate student divulges, *"thinks I'm lazy because Laotian women are supposed to get up early, cook and take care of the house, and I don't have the time to do those things. I am working to take my family out of poverty, but it is unimaginable to them."*

On the other hand, Evan took a semester off at the start of junior year. A good friend had been murdered. His concentration slipped. His parents had health problems; he wanted to help. One semester became three years. *"I knew I had to return but it was very hard going back."* He and a high school classmate who also took a break that ended up being several years give advice contrary to what they did: *"Once you start, don't stop. Press on. You can do it."* Both these guys show you can pause and return, and sometimes, circumstances make that the wise choice. But if you really want to be in school, work to stay there.

Here is advice our interviewees told us to write over and over: Seek out input from others. (Go back and look again at Chapter 3, **Everyone's #1 Piece of Advice**.) When you have to make a major decision, find a faculty member or administrator on campus or maybe somebody you know outside of school that you consider wise. Choose people that you think can listen to you and appreciate your situation. Be open and honest about the issues you face. It may lead you to see the issue in a different way. *"When I got a research job, and my boss became my mentor and then friend and I could speak openly, everything got easier,"* Cara says.

To ask for advice, it is much easier if you already know who that person is, which is why we hope throughout this book you heed the advice of those ahead of you telling you to: **Get to know faculty. Get to know administrators. Find mentors. Find allies.** You do not have to take any offered advice, but many times an outsider can give you a clearer perspective or suggest a different strategy. Give it a chance. After all, isn't one of the things we are supposed to learn in college is how to improve our communication skills?

Not everyone will be helpful. Savannah is still pained by being rejected from a teaching program because *"This White woman interviewed me and wouldn't recommend me because she said my accent was too thick to teach."* She is telling this story in easily understandable, lightly accented English. But she also has stories about the many people, bosses, teachers, friends, who helped her in her decade-long journey from welfare to a graduate degree. *"I wouldn't be here without all the people who went out of their way to ease my difficulties."*

Roberto says his community college mentor, part of a formal California state program aimed at helping to alleviate the educational barriers that keep students from going to college called ESOP (Extended Opportunity Program Services), was essential in helping him manage his first two years at a community college and then with his transfer to a four-year state school. *"My best advice for any First Gen is to find an experienced person who can help."*

TAKE ACTION

Think now about to whom you could turn if you needed help in thinking through a family problem. If you can't identify someone, can you name a person you would like to work on knowing better who could become a sounding board?

RURAL STUDENTS

Rural students are less likely to attend college than their urban or suburban counterparts. Forty-two percent of people ages 18 to 24 are enrolled in all of higher education; only 29 percent of rural people in that age group are enrolled, compared with nearly 48 percent from cities.

Lee, the young woman from rural Idaho, remembers growing up not knowing anyone who went to college. *"This was a Mormon town of 1200, and girls especially were not supposed to go to college. Because I was White, people were more likely to assume I knew what was going on at college, but, in fact, I had no idea how dorms worked or classes were chosen, and I was too ashamed to ask for help."*

Rural students may pass up high quality schools that offer them generous financial aid, choosing, like many other First Generation children, to stay close to home. They worry about city crime, feeling lost in the busyness of a big school, and finding themselves where they know no one. And if many low-income working-class parents, those who may have never been able to attend high school, insist on college because they want their kids to "do better," some rural parents have an opposite view:

> Fewer rural White men are convinced that colleges and universities have a role in providing necessary skills . . . 71% think they do, compared with 82% of urban and 84% of suburban White men.

> This has become a cultural phenomenon. It's not an educational phenomenon . . . Encouraging a rural student to go

to college instead of doing the same work as the adults in a community . . . is like suggesting that the child should not do what I have done, should not be where I have been, should not value all that I have raised them to honor, whether that's going to the mill or turning on the tractor at 6 a.m.[11]

TAKE ACTION

Step back and look at your family as an outsider. What are the strengths you see in your family? How have they contributed to you being in college? How did their upbringing contribute to who they are as parents?

11 https://hechingerreport.org/high-school-grads-least-likely-america-go-college-rural-ones/

11 https://hechingerreport.org/high-school-grads-least-likely-america-go-college-rural-ones/

FAMILY OF CHOICE

So far, we have been talking about biological families. Going out into the world affords us the opportunity to forge another kind of family—a family of choice. A family of choice is bound by voluntary commitments. These are people who may not share our genes, but do share a deep affection and appreciation for one another. They feel like kin in spirit. We may have a greater sense of intimacy with these people than with birth family members.

Families of choice can provide a kind of support and comfort we are missing, or they can complement whatever we already have, especially if we are far away from our families. These will only be people who make you feel good about yourself, people you enjoy spending time with. They don't always have to agree with you, but they won't demean you when they don't agree. They don't always have to be available, but you have to feel comfortable asking when they are. They don't have to look like you or act like you, or be your age or ethnicity, but they have to listen to you and you to them.

Families of choice often come together over meals. Have a dinner party for people you care about. Don't worry about how big your room is, how small your kitchen is. Sit on the floor. Use paper plates. Ask everyone to bring something. Light some candles, kidnap some greenery from outside. Talk, laugh, enjoy. On special occasions, give gifts. The gifts don't have to cost anything. Share a playlist. Download a poem. Bake cookies. Give a "ticket" for an errand, a ride, a favor. This kind of familial intimacy may happen in a sudden burst of connection, but usually it happens slowly, over time as we learn what there is to value in the people we know.

To forge this kind of relationship, each person is a giver and a taker. The glue is the desire to be kind and helpful to one another. It happens in small acts. You put your phone down during a conversation. You send a check-in message when you know something big has happened for your friend. You don't make promises you can't keep. You are honest in what you say and kind in how you say it. And you expect all that in return.

We can have lots of friends, but family by choice is a special category of friend. These friendships can last for decades, or they can fall away with time and distance, but they are fulfilling in the moment. Especially if you feel your own family doesn't get you, look for people who do.

TAKE ACTION

For the next holiday on the calendar, can you imagine hosting a small gathering for people you think are special? Is there someone you'd like to ask to help you organize a gathering?

Get involved in a college organization or activity that makes it easy to know people. Maybe it's a social club, a sports team, an arts group or a volunteer activity. Find something that connects you closely to others.

6

THE IMPORTANCE OF EMOTIONAL WELL-BEING

ANXIETY AND DEPRESSION

The First Gen interviews confirmed the research findings: when our mental well-being is out of kilter, it hampers our ability to function well academically or professionally. An outstanding student with a full scholarship to an outstanding school recalls how she initially stumbled:

> It was such a competitive environment. Everybody is so focused on grades and getting things perfectly. You have been outstanding all your life, and suddenly you are not the best. Anxiety starts popping up. And then once you get anxious about school, you find you are anxious about everything. And then you start feeling paralyzed.

Another student, in a large multi-cultural state school, was done in by different pressures:

> I just try to succeed at everything I do, and I felt like I needed to prove myself—at work and at school. I was living alone and had all these bills to pay so I kept working more. There was pressure from so many directions. I did get counseling and thought I was doing all the right things, and then I cracked.

Yes, everybody has up days and down days. Feeling sad or low sometimes is part of life. But when those feelings won't go away, when you are persistently sad and uncomfortable in your own skin, when your normal patterns suddenly are replaced by sleeping or eating or mood disruptions, it's time to ask if you are slipping into a clinical depression.

Depression, sadly, is pervasive in all college students. A 2019 report from the American College Health Association found that in the past year, 87% of college students felt overwhelmed by all they had to do, 66% felt overwhelming anxiety, 56% felt things were hopeless and 13% seriously considered suicide. But First Generation students have an enhanced risk for depression, especially if they are people of color. **Being aware of the risk; finding people who won't let you forget your self-worth is important protection.**

SIGNS OF DEPRESSION

- Trouble concentrating, remembering details, and making decisions
- Feelings of guilt, worthlessness, and helplessness
- Pessimism and hopelessness
- Insomnia, early-morning wakefulness, or sleeping too much
- Irritability
- Restlessness
- Loss of interest in things once pleasurable, including sex
- Overeating, or appetite loss
- Aches, pains, headaches, or cramps that won't go away
- Digestive problems that don't get better, even with treatment
- Persistent sad, anxious, or "empty" feelings
- Suicidal thoughts or attempts

If you factor in poverty and racism on top of normal coming-of-age pressures, feeling bad is easy. Then, making it tougher, minority students and those who feel on the "outside" often think they need to keep their difficulties to themselves. Seventy-five percent of Black students report keeping their feelings private, compared to 61% of White students. [12] But other cultures also stigmatize mental health. A computer science major talks about ending up on suicide watch in the hospital and being sent home because her college judged her to be a danger to herself before her South-Asian parents could open up to discussing mental health.

Feeling the pressures of social differences, the consequences of little money, and the constant hum of unease can have serious physical effects.

"Weathering the cumulative effects of living in a society characterized by White dominance and privilege produces a kind of physical and mental wear-and-tear that contributes to a host of psychological and physical ailments," explains Ebony McGee, an assistant professor of diversity and urban schooling at Vanderbilt and co-author of a recent study on Black students and mental health. . . . The study, whose analysis is based on critical race theory, explores how racism affects the ability of high-achieving Black students[13] to have healthy mental attitudes toward their

---

12 While this study specifies Black students, our interviews suggest this work applies to other minorities and to low-income First Generation students in general. Caucasian students are not immune to feeling low self-esteem. White students from rural areas notably can experience acute culture shock in urban colleges.

13 While this study specifies Black students, our interviews suggest this work applies to other minorities and to low-income First Generation students in general. Caucasian students are not immune to feeling low self-esteem. White students from rural areas notably can experience acute culture shock in urban colleges.

work and college experiences. "We have documented alarming occurrences of anxiety, stress, depression and thoughts of suicide, as well as a host of physical ailments like hair loss, diabetes and heart disease," she writes.[14]

One value of looking at research around minority student mental health is to appreciate how circumstances can be structural and not personal. You, a single individual, do not bear the burden of your pains alone. Rather, the whole culture has gotten screwed up, and it may be landing on you but not because of you.

It can alleviate some feelings of distress if you appreciate how "normal" it is to feel "not normal" or stressed. Dr. Mc Gee and her co-author Dr. David Stovall, an associate professor of African American studies and educational policy at University of Illinois at Chicago, found this:

> We have grown accustomed to talking about grit, perseverance, and mental toughness without properly acknowledging the multiple forms of suffering [Black students] have confronted (and still confront) as part of that story . . . Colleges rely on all the positive aspects of grit to define the "college experience" by paying attention only to its static definition: courage, resolve, the innate ability to bounce back from obstacles. But history, the researchers argue, has shown that the types of institutional biases that are at play in the U.S. education system are structured to devalue the work of students of color, which can't be fixed with an extra dose of mental toughness.

---

14 https://www.theatlantic.com/education/archive/2016/01/balancing-academia-racism/424887/

. . . we have witnessed Black students work themselves to the point of extreme illness in attempting to escape the constant threat (treadmill) of perceived intellectual inferiority. However, what grit researchers do not adequately examine is the role that race plays in producing anxiety, trauma, and general unpleasantness in students of color engaging in high-pressure academic work. The psychological and emotional energy required to manage stress in academic and social contexts as well as systemic and everyday racism can be overwhelming and taxing.

Worsening these challenges, students of color are less likely than their White counterparts to seek and undergo psychological treatment—a disparity that *The Wall Street Journal* has reported is widespread on elite college campuses. Barriers to seeking care—such as cost, lack of availability, and the stigmas associated with therapy—combined with a mistrust of the healthcare system and racism, contribute to the gap, according to a supplement to the Surgeon General's 1999 report on mental health. That Black students utilize mental-health services much less may also reflect a cultural mistrust of the universities, according to some research. The racism that students experience on their campuses suggests that colleges and universities are systems that perpetuate their pain. "So, going to a counseling center within a university that perpetuates institutional racism is just kind of like a conflict of interest for many students," McGee says.[15]

15 https://www.theatlantic.com/education/archive/2016/01/balancing-academia-racism/424887/

Feelings of invisibility that make students feel invalidated and microaggressions which can cause racial battle fatigue are triggers for depression. Finding people who understand the feelings you have and can validate them, whether in the counseling center or elsewhere, is important. It is one reason students value having dedicated campus spaces for First Generation students, students of color, and other groups that can be marginalized. A young woman who helped to start a First Generation student organization on her campus remembers feeling . . . ". . . there was no place on campus where I could speak authentically and feel understood. Too often, my peers were just not receptive to my issues. They couldn't relate to my world."

LISTEN TO WHAT THOSE WHO HAVE BEEN THROUGH CLINICAL DEPRESSION HAVE TO SAY:

From a book of personal narratives, volume I, compiled by the TRIO Student Support Services at Indiana University Purdue University Fort Wayne (IPFW)

I never imagined I would be in the hospital over something as simple as stress from school and work. It scared me to know that something that simple could hurt me so much. But it didn't just scare me. It taught me. It taught me that there are resources beyond simple tutoring. It taught me that support offered by the university for its students was not just there for show. And perhaps most important, it taught me to take the time to use those resources and keep myself mentally and physically healthy.

Every Student Has A Story. Marty Herrick, p. 76

I had many struggles as everyone does with learning routines, figuring out professors, and getting used to the workload of each class. As so many people do, I also struggled with depression and anxiety and found myself wanting to drop out by the end of first year. Many friends I had met dropped out of school and this made me question if I wanted to be there . . .

. . . Although I made mistakes and now know there were probably better ways to handle my decisions over the years, along the way, I learned the importance of not being afraid to ask questions or make those mistakes. I learned to always just keep moving forward without letting the fear of the unknown stop me.

Every Student Has A Story. Abigail Wiegand, pp. 67-68

Often times I find myself stressed out now that I'm in my first year of college. Fortunately, my drive for school is back. . . . It's awesome to have knowledge, but in those times when stress does hit, a piece of advice for myself and all those reading this, is to talk about it. A closed mouth does not get fed. You do not have to handle everything on your own. It is not you who makes you super, it is those around you who give you that ability.

Every Student Has A Story. Jo'Male Collie p. 36

This doesn't mean everyone will hit a bump, but should you and a serious bump collide, please do not hesitate to look for and ask for help. Based on all we have learned working on this book, **thinking it is weak or wrong to ask for help is both common and extremely unhelpful.** There is ample evidence that finds having others validate our experiences reduces lasting trauma.

If you find stress is causing you to crater academically, absolutely make an appointment with your professor(s) and/or advisor. You may need an extension or an explanation or a direction or just some adult reassurance. This is part of their academic job. It is not weak to do this. It is normal. *"I didn't visit a faculty member in his office until my junior year,"* explained an Ivy League graduate. *"I wasn't sure what I was supposed to say. Now I know there are not special code words."*

We can't promise every faculty member will give you what you need—there are many stories of professors who are insensitive or demeaning—but try. They will not eat you. Explain what is happening and ask for advice about how to handle your situation. If you don't feel understood, pick someone else. Just because someone has a Ph.D. does not mean he or she has empathy. Many, many students, however, report finding sympathetic, helpful faculty. Just being heard, saying what is on your mind aloud when you are alone, is helpful.

Find a counselor or a staff person you have come to trust and allow yourself to be vulnerable. Admit that you are on shaky ground and need some anchoring. Tai almost dropped out at the end of his first month of college:

" I struggled my entire fucking first year. I didn't understand the reading. I tried to do it all myself. I didn't trust anybody and then, my fourth week, when I was ready to drop out, it just hit me that maybe I didn't have to do it all myself anymore. I made an appointment with this woman who runs the Asian American student association. She really helped me. She made me see I was normal, and she gave me all these resources I didn't know about. I didn't even know such a thing as an LGBTQ group existed. "

If your campus has a program that focuses on First Generation students, multiculturalism, or diversity, get connected. There are thousands of student support programs at colleges and universities around the country to support First Gens. Lots of research shows that when students participate in these programs, their grades and their graduation rates go up. Often their satisfaction with college goes up too. If you have an office called TRIO on campus, find a way to engage if you feel isolated or pressured.

A freshman at a big state school looks back on her first year, and that of a good friend. *"She hardly ever left the dorm, feeling this pressure to study all the time. I got involved in clubs and found it made classes easier because that's how I connected to study groups, got tips from upper classmen and relaxed."* She wants you to know that those first few weeks of school is the time to look for campus organizations. *"There are all sorts of events that are easy to access, and upper classmen remember what it's like and are super-friendly. It's before you have to worry about mid-terms. Most schools have culture clubs where you can find people who share your cultural inheritance. Oh, and the clubs often have food, too, if you are hungry."*

If you are struggling with mental health issues, there are two additional resources outside your college. We don't have personal experience with either, but they are free and easily accessible.

https://www.stevefund.org/VeqPXgdy7Zw4Ezwm748/
(see their programs and services)

https://www.7cups.com/
(free online therapy for students)

Many times, that feeling of anxiety or depression is deepened by feeling ashamed of being weak, of not having it all together. And even without depression, shame is triggered by all kinds of signals other people don't even know they are sending. So, let's look at shame.

TAKE ACTION

Write down the names of two people (or more) you think can provide support and guidance when you are feeling overwhelmed. If you have not connected with these people, write down when and how you can make that connection.

Set up regular check-ins with people who help you feel centered. Touch base in good times as well as hard times.

SHAME AND VULNERABILITY

Dr. Brené Brown is an expert on shame. She has felt it, researched it, written and talked about it, and helped many of us see that the roots of many behaviors that get in our way are seated in shame.

Brown says that shame is our belief that if other people know or see us as we are, they won't want to connect with us. "Shame," explains Brown, "is underpinned by the feeling, I'm not good enough." Many college students find themselves feeling not good enough, but it is especially acute with First Generation students who are dealing with multiple shifts in what they previously presumed to be reality.

Guilt and shame are different emotions. **Guilt is about behavior. It says what I did is not good enough. Shame says I am not good enough. It is a focus on self. And it turns out that guilt leads to positive, adaptive behaviors while shame can seduce us into self-harming actions.**

The antidote? It's not studying more, drinking more, or dressing better. This one is free. Any student can have it and use it: It is, simply—or maybe it's not really so simple—the courage to be imperfect.

Here is what Dr. Brown pulled from her years of shame research: **Shame is rooted in vulnerability. Feeling vulnerable makes us wobbly and uncomfortable. But it is "the birthplace of creativity, innovation and change."**

To be vulnerable takes courage, the courage to let ourselves be seen by the world—and by ourselves—as imperfect. We are all imperfect, and those who deny this, who try to project an image of perfection, turn out to be annoying to others. There is an inauthenticity to that which saps the energy of the seemingly perfect person, but also of those around them.

If someone has told you that going off to college was meant to be an exercise in vulnerability, would you really have wanted to leave your bedroom? But what if we can convince you that embracing vulnerability is a big, fat, free key to success? It is what allows us to move into new spaces with feeling like an imposter.

TAKE ACTION

Find 20 minutes, get a cup of coffee and listen to Dr. Brown's first TED Talks.[16] Type TED Talks, Brené Brown in your browser. Look for the Talk called *Listening to Shame*.

If you find it helpful, you might want to listen to the second one on the power of vulnerability.[17]

16 https://www.ted.com/talks/brene_brown_listening_to_shame?language=en
17 https://www.ted.com/talks/brene_brown_the_power_of_vulnerability?language=en#t-1200187

A PARTIAL LIST OF REASONS FIRST GENS GIVE FOR FEELING SHAME

"I'm in school while my siblings are not."

"I'm a fraud. I don't really belong here."

"My family is sacrificing for me, and I'll fail them."

"I don't want people to know who I really am, where I'm really from."

"Someone else deserves these opportunities more than me."

"I feel a growing distance from my family, but I know they love me."

"I didn't really earn this. I was just lucky to be born smart."

"My peers don't really know who I am, and I don't want them to know."

"I don't really have anything interesting to contribute."

"Here I am, and I cannot figure this out."

"If I speak up, I'll sound foolish and/or dumb."

"I can't keep up with my peers."

"I should feel grateful, but I feel mad/sad/angry/fearful."

If you are convinced, here are six things you might consider in order to exercise your vulnerability chops:

1. Visit at least two professors during office hours. Come up with two questions and go with the intention of simply developing a relationship.

2. Invite someone you find interesting, but don't really know, to coffee, a walk, a campus event.

3. Share with a roommate or friend something about yourself that you have been hiding (unless, maybe, it's illegal).

4. Ask for help regarding something that has been bothering you.

5. Let people know what you dream about doing. Say it out loud.

6. Make a friend with someone you think is NOT like you.

TAKE ACTION

Look at the list above and commit to doing one thing on the list.

USE MENTAL HEALTH TOOLS ON YOUR PHONE

Falling apart can happen like a ceiling collapse. Something has slowly been dripping through the plaster, weakening it bit by bit, until one day it just caves in on you. Every student who has experienced a cave-in will tell you to pay attention to the signs and look for help. Negative emotions and constant stress drain your battery, and when the battery has no more juice, we come to a halt.

"I was," Amara says *"the perfect Indian child. I had good grades. I won awards, went to the White House science fair, had my own patents."* She was eager to go away for college and chose a university with an excellent engineering program a couple of states distant. *". . . And I did really poorly my first two years. Then, the beginning of my third year, I was in and out of the hospital until I ended up in the ER on a ventilator for trying to kill myself."* The school required she drop out, and she went home for 18 months.

"Indian families don't discuss mental health issues. I could never talk to my parents before this happened about what I was feeling." Amara says she had no coping strategies and felt increasingly isolated. It was only after she was driven to such a drastic act that she was diagnosed with bi-polar disorder.

At home, working on recovery, Amara decided to use her own experiences and her skills in computer science to do something to help others. *"After you have a crisis, you can get help developing a coping plan, but you also need to have a crisis plan in place before the crisis."*

She developed a free online app called **Anenome** especially for college students that can help them prepare a mental health plan in advance of a crisis and to help them or their peers or parents locate immediate resources in the middle of a crisis. It can be accessed from the App store for iPhones.

Amara is now back on her campus and deeply involved in helping her school develop better ways to help students with mental health issues. She has found that using apps to manage stress helps students. Many online tools have a modest monthly cost, but two are currently free. Take a look at **https://woebot.io/**. Well-trained psychologists have used artificial intelligence (AI) technology and the principles of cognitive-based therapy to allow you to address mood issues any time, any place. Although you are not talking to a real person, reviews say the site is helpful.

The best rated site is **www.sanvello.com**. There is a free version or an expanded version for $9/month. A review of the site[18] says:

> In a randomized study of 500 adults with mild to moderate anxiety and depression, the tools offered by Sanvello were shown to decrease symptoms. The effects lasted even after participants stopped using the app. Sanvello provides users with cognitive behavioral therapy tools.

One meditation and sleep app that has hundreds of good reviews is **www.headspace.com**. Students can sign up for $10/year and, among other things, receive a short daily meditation. Not many interviewees spoke about meditation, but the research is rich

---

18 https://www.verywellmind.com/best-mental-health-apps-4692902

with descriptions of its centering benefits. Or take a look at **www.calm.com**, another meditation site that gets high marks. It's free for the first week and then about $70/year so you can try it and see if you find it useful. (See the section on *Mindfulness and Meditation* in **Taking Care of Yourself**, Chapter 9.)

Another free site is **www.daylio.net**. This is a mood tracker that lets you follow your patterns and test out what strategies seem to have an impact for you.

TAKE ACTION

If you worry about managing your moods, do you want to check out the sites recommended above so you will have a place to turn if there is a need? Could you stop and do it now?

7

MONEY

IT SUCKS TO BE POOR

Okay, let's just get it out right up front: it sucks to be poor. About 27% of First Generation students come from families making $20,000 or less, compared to 6% of non-First Generation students. The median income for First Generation freshmen at two- and four-year colleges was $37,563 compared with $99,635 for non-First Generation freshmen. Not all First Generation students come from low-income families. Some come from affluence, but those students who do not have parents who were able to receive an education and do not have family resources dominate the current First Gen pool. Consequently, many First Generation students are worrying about how to manage school costs, living costs, and even help for their families.

One First Gen college professor working with First Gen students concluded: "In 2020, you can be Black and be proud. You can be gay and be proud. You can't be poor and be proud. Poverty makes you feel shameful over your parents' failure to achieve the American dream."

That's a grim statement. We put it out here so we can stare it in the face and talk about it. Shame is something no one can give you. We have to allow it ourselves, and we want to do our best to inoculate you against shame. (See the section on *Shame* in Chapter 6.) Researchers have begun to talk about the lasting trauma that poverty can bring.[19]

19 https://medium.com/@duequach/poor-and-traumatized-at-harvard-e5938b702207

Stacy, who is now in grad school, showed up on a small liberal arts campus with many affluent students. *"I never told anyone I was First Generation or sought out institutional help because I didn't want to limit myself with that label. It made me feel ashamed. Now I know that wasn't good for me."*

THE CONSEQUENCES OF GOING TO COLLEGE POOR CAN HIT IN DIFFERENT WAYS:

1. You know about tuition, but you are unprepared for the costs of fees and books.

2. You have tuition covered, but still must deal with food and housing and you may need to deal with it during vacations as well when dorms are closed.

3. How do you manage for all those little things and get-togethers with classmates or friends that can involve spending money, often on food or transportation?

4. How do you manage travel to and from home?

5. How do you balance the need to work for money with the need to study?

6. What do you do when your family has expenses they can't cover, and they want your help?

7. How do you manage not being able to afford going out with friends? Do you just say you can't afford it? Would you be comfortable if they paid? Do you just make up an excuse?

8. When you are deciding on a major, should future earning potential be part of your equation?

9. Is it an issue when you cannot purchase clothing that is popular on campus or attend cultural events that cost money?

10. Are you tempted to make decisions you know are poor for short-term gain?

11. Do you put your health at risk by trying to save money on food?

That's a lot of issues to juggle while also juggling the normal concerns of college students.

Maybe it's akin to having extra rocks in your backpack, stealing your energy and attention even if not consciously. And from all that we have been told, students do experience embarrassment, shame, feelings of low self-worth and anger connected with circumstances that make them feel poor. **But low income is an economic condition only. It is not a reflection of ability, character or attitude.**

There is also this fierce drive and determination that is both gift and danger. *"My parents,"* a 21-year-old woman tells us, *"are Mexican immigrants who have very little education, and they taught me and my three siblings to work hard for what we want. I have always felt the need to prove myself in every situation."*

With that script in her brain, Rose started college overwhelmed by the strangeness of her big urban university, working a full-time job, heart-broken from a romantic breakup and taking four classes that she wasn't quite sure how she had chosen. In spite of graduating in the top ten percent of her high school class, Rose failed three of her four classes that first semester.

Determined to get back in her groove, she doubled down on everything, working harder at work and at school. She was a classic case of John Henryism, that urge to be perfect, and she kept working harder and harder. By the start of her third year, broken by all the pressures she felt, she ended up in the psych ward. She was forced to drop out for that semester and then stay out another semester. Her low GPA cost her eligibility for financial aid. This is the point where many students just give up. Rose would not give up. She is back in school, living at home an hour away from the university, taking three classes, working three days a week and thinking about how to get to graduate school. Money is always on her mind, and the lack of it makes life more complicated, but she has learned that always pushing to make more money is not her best bet for success.

All sorts of unanticipated events can trip us up. You can get sick and have to miss more days of work than you planned. You can lose your winter coat and need to buy a new one. You find out you have to spend money on medical care you didn't expect. We know this stuff throws you off balance. Remember, the abnormal is really pretty normal. The world is not picking on you. Glitches happen to everyone—it just is so much harder when every penny counts. Again, go for advice. Ask for help. Some schools have emergency funds for students in crisis. You may have grown up feeling that you could only depend on yourself, but now you have support structures put in place to help, and it's okay to use them. You don't have to do this alone.

The majority of interviews took place in the spring of 2020 as the coronavirus was shutting down schools across the country and forcing them to transition to online classes. We hope you are reading this when this crisis has passed, and schools are re-opened. But if you are in an acute financial situation down the line, consider taking a semester of online classes so you can have more flexible work hours, but make sure the credits will be accepted by your school. Don't just quit—arrange a leave, a formal period of absence that allows you to return; be sure you understand how you will be able to return when you are ready. Talk with your advisor and with the registrar.

Over 60% of all college students find themselves short of money at some point in college. Fifty-four percent of first-time college students leave without a degree because they say they could not afford to continue, versus 45% of continuing generation students.[20]

Here is where you have to get very serious with yourself. Ask yourself: Do I want to drop out because the money issues are stressful? Is it because you are not sure you belong in college now? Or do you really know you belong in college, but money is a serious problem? If you know you belong, now is the time to commit to figuring out, one way or another, how you will get your college degree. If you can't have the ideal college experience, if you can't just study and socialize, okay, too bad, but don't let the dream die. Use every resource you can find, every strategy possible to get that degree. Khalid, who works with disadvantaged high schoolers, tells me to write: *"It is more important to accept your circumstances and properly prepare to succeed than to be continually unsatisfied and holding back your full efforts or being stretched thin trying to have it all."*

---

20 https://www.goodcall.com/news/over-60-of-college-students-have-run-out-of-money-during-a-semester-reveals-new-survey-05538/

HUNGRY OR HOMELESS OR HOPELESS

Around 60% of students, especially community college students, experience food insecurity sometimes. They are hungry and can't afford food. If you find yourself in this situation, make sure you are taking advantage of all the public and private support systems available to you like SNAP and food pantries. **Many students do not take advantage of the benefits to which they are entitled.** Consider finding a job that involves food and shares some with staff. Look for campus events where food is being served. Pick up community newspapers in the student commons and look for coupons. Find out if there is a campus food pantry or nearby community pantries. Do not let a fear of feeling stigmatized keep you away from free food. Hunger gets in the way of studying and staying balanced. Taking care of yourself makes you smart, not needy.

Some students also deal with homelessness. If this is you, this is, for sure, a time to ask for help. Trying to do well in school, do well at work, be homeless and hungry is an impossible circumstance that you should not endure alone. The world brought this to you. Let's try to get the community to help you solve it.

Sometimes, it makes sense to find a less expensive way to go to college or even take a break, but before you do, talk to yourself; be sure you are not using money as the excuse for other difficulties that can be addressed without money. Everybody does not belong in college. Everybody doesn't need a degree. However, people with a college degree usually earn more and have more career options. And people who have gotten a college degree tend to be better at learning how to learn and gaining insight into themselves and others who are different from them. There is a national discussion now about aiming for 60% of Americans to have some sort of post-secondary education.

If you do decide to leave college—although the point of this whole book is to help you graduate—have a plan. Figure out what you want to do and what preparation you need to get there. **If you are going to quit, quit FOR something, not because it feels too tough.**

TREAT LEARNING ABOUT FINANCIAL AID LIKE A PART-TIME JOB

Nope, can't rob a bank or print dollars in the library. How we wish! Let's hope and pray public policy will lead us to tuition-free college options. Until then, there isn't an easy answer and most of the interviews we had included conversations about money. But they also showed the many different ways people figured out how to fund their education.

Know money can be a stressor. Certainly, lack of money is a pain in the ass. A good strategy is to invest time in reading about financial aid, in understanding the different kinds of loans and the varied choices you have for choosing a college. Treat learning about financial aid like a part-time job, one that pays you later instead of now. It's complicated and filling out the key financial aid form, FAFSA (Free Application For Student Aid) and various scholarship forms require an understanding of the "right" ways to complete them. Check out the FAFSA online suggestions.[21] The starting place for FAFSA is the government site which has lots of useful, straightforward information. Just type "studentaid. gov" into your browser. Unless you are independent, you will need your parents to participate in filling out the form. Several students reported serious difficulties in getting parental help. *"My sister and I found that begging, pestering, daily calls and generally being super annoying was our best strategy."*

---

21 https://www.nasfaa.org/fafsa_tips

Look for people who understand FAFSA and ask for help.[22] Be open to considering colleges that are not nearby, maybe even several states away. Are you willing to risk leaving home and maybe some bouts of homesickness for less debt and maybe a more satisfying education at a school far way? Khalid was an outstanding southern California high school student who thought as a kid he would go to an Ivy League college. On paper, he looked like a good candidate for a full scholarship ride somewhere. But when it came time to apply to schools, he only applied to University of California campuses. He's been a star on his campus and is happy, but he did not get complete funding and worked *"way too many hours freshman year. It hurt my grades, and it made me unhappy."* Why didn't he apply more broadly? *"Well . . . truthfully, I was afraid of rejection."* Jerrie had full scholarship offers outside her home state but wanted to stay close to home. It was a good idea to be able to come home when school felt overwhelming, but now she regrets ending up with $36,000 in debt.

When looking at financial aid, you may be offered a package with both loans and grants. Know the difference. Grants are gifts. You don't have to pay them back although you may have to maintain a certain grade point level. Loans are money you will have to pay back with interest after you leave school. Having a large loan obligation can keep you from being able to get credit for big ticket items like cars or houses. Make sure you understand how you will have to pay back loans.

---

22 Filing the FAFSA (fafsa.ed.gov) each year by the priority filing deadline set by the school the student attends. Many students miss out on funds because they don't file on time or at all. It's never too late to file, even midterm. Students who file the FAFSA in January, February and March tend to receive twice as much grant aid. New forms are posted in October for the coming school year.

TAKE ACTION

Get a good fix on what money comes as a grant and what comes as a loan and how you will have to pay it back. If you are accepting a loan, calculate your total debt by the end of college. Write down some questions you can ask the financial aid office about other ways to improve the offer with less debt. Make an appointment with the financial aid office to ask your questions.

FIRST THE RAIN,
THEN THE RAINBOW

Lack of money is not one thing; it's a continuum. Students on full scholarships at elite schools have one category of money problems. They may not need to worry about tuition, but they are constantly in situations where not having discretionary income makes them feel out of place. How do you remember that you are doing the campus a favor by bringing your different way of seeing the world when friends are suggesting activities you cannot afford, and you wonder if you belong?

Jane said, "*I would tell myself that is part of the cost of getting a college degree and it's really the easy part. Usually, I would say, 'I would love to come but I have to work then or study for an exam.'*"

Hector said, "*I tried only to be good friends with poor kids.*"

Felton brashly told friends "*You know if I come, you gotta pay for it because I'm stone broke so only ask if you are treating.*"

Shauna kept her stash. "*I just worked at always having a $10 bill that I would resist using for other stuff so I could sometimes go for coffee or pizza. I shopped at the Goodwill so I could keep that little bit of play money.*"

Jamie likes lightness and humor in difficult situations. Money issues, she said, revolved around eating out, and her response was, "*Oh no, you know those college budgets we all have. Mine just won't let me do this now.*"

Odds are, it's going to happen. There are going to be moments when you just can't afford something no one else seems to think about. Maybe you find a lack of travel money keeps you stuck on campus like Coral. *"My friend and I couldn't go home one Thanksgiving, but we forgot that everything would be closed Thanksgiving Day, and we were too embarrassed to let anyone know we were going to be alone on campus. We ended up at McDonald's for Thanksgiving dinner. It was so bleak, we pledged to each other we would never speak of it."* It's hard to have to worry about money constantly, but it might help a little to remind yourself that many students with money in their pockets did not earn that money. They may enjoy it, but it is not a sign of merit, only good fortune. If the money in your pocket came from your hard work, give yourself credit for that.

If you have a close group of intimate friends, perhaps there will be a moment when you can discuss the challenges of insufficient resources. It is a gift to help people who have never experienced this realize that low income is perfectly compatible with being smart, hard-working, well-meaning and good hearted. People can be stuck in low-earning jobs because they were given no education, no expectations and no breaks, and/or because illness or hardship or bad luck were factors in their lives. Families living in economic poverty can be rich in warmth and laughter, and affluence cannot buy that. And then people may also be without resources because their parents made foolish choices that they are working to avoid. **You may be money-broke for now but being in college means you are already growing rich in other ways**.

At the other end of the continuum are students from low income backgrounds who don't have enough financial aid to cover college costs or don't have any aid at all. They are not worried about buying a latte. They are worried about paying the rent or keeping gas in the car that gets them to college. They are working full-time jobs while going to school. Maybe they are living at home and trying to help their parents, or they are living in apartments where they have to pay for light, heat and cable. Maybe they have kids. They are very tired people. If this is you, recognize that for the next few years, you are a juggler, having to juggle competing priorities. One ball is always going to be up in the air, and sometimes, balls will drop.

Isella is one amazing juggler. Pregnant at 18, divorced with two kids at 28, she fell into a for-profit program in electronics and computer technology that promised a fast associates degree and a job within six months of graduation. The promise was false and the education sub-standard. The $20,000 debt was real. She figured out how to get a paralegal degree from the community college while working full-time and then filled in the basic core academic requirements for a four-year degree. She transferred to the University of Houston Downtown for a degree in criminal justice that she could take entirely online, which was all she could manage with a heavy workload and children. How did she do it? *"The hardest part was finding time to study. But I feel like if you are really interested in the subject, you will learn enough. If you are not really interested, you will make excuses. If you really like what you are doing, it's easy. You just do it."*

If Isella is an example of how much one can manage, Rose's breakdown, discussed above, is a warning for what can happen if you get so tired, so pressured and anxious, that all the balls come tumbling down on top of you. It can happen to people who are sure they can cope.

HERE ARE SOME STRATEGIES INTERVIEWEES SUGGEST FOR MANAGING MONEY ISSUES

- Don't let the need for money let you neglect the education you came to get.

- Consider whether you can get a better financial deal by leaving home or your home state. Be open to all sorts of options.

- Ask yourself when it makes sense to take time out to earn money and when it makes sense to risk more debt. Then ask someone else who has some experience with this so you can be sure you are thinking clearly. Check in with the financial aid and work-study staff on your campus.

- It's not a good financial deal to lose scholarship aid because you work so hard that your grades drop. It may make sense not to work one semester and take more than 15 hours and then to work hard the next semester and, if you won't lose aid, take 9 hours or even six. Are there some classes you can take online for credit so that you can squeeze them into your schedule?

- Can you find free room and board by living with a family that needs childcare or home maintenance help?

- Is it better to work on campus for less money than commuting back and forth for a bit more?

- Can you save enough money to ease your burden if you take a semester off to work full-time, or will that distract you from graduating?

- Apply for every scholarship you can and make sure you talk with the financial aid and work study offices on your campus.

- Go to your community college for your first two years because it will be the least expensive option; but excel and apply to transfer to a four-year school that will offer you a good aid package for your last two years.

Rene got to college because she became part of a program in eighth grade aimed at directing low income students to college. *"They made me aware of college and taught us all the things you need to know to apply."* But she feels the program didn't do a good job of explaining loans and what that would mean long term. *"Had I truly understood what I was doing with my loans, I would have gone to a community college for two years and then transferred to a four-year school."* Now Rene has $30,000 in debt and she is struggling as a creative writing major to find her career path.

Diabetes is a chronic condition. Until we have a medical breakthrough, it won't go away. Asthma is a chronic condition and so is arthritis. Poverty does not need to be chronic. You don't have to experience poverty in the future. That's why you are focusing on your education. This is your temporary state of being. You can stress over money—or you can worry, but also remember that you are working toward more options in life. You didn't choose your height or your eye color. And you can't change them. **You didn't choose your poverty, but in time, you can change this one, so be patient.** Hang in there. It will pass.

TAKE ACTION

Is there one thing you would really like to have that you deny yourself? (We are thinking in the under $50 category here, not the guitar or the Porsche.) Put a jar in your underwear drawer and every time you've got some change you can spare or have a few extra dollars, put it in the jar and then, after the next set of exams, just go treat yourself.

WORKING WHILE GOING TO SCHOOL

Every student interviewed but one who was still a freshman and had a complete package that left her with some spending money, worked some time while in college. Some worked as few as eight hours a week and some worked full-time. Each situation is different and each person's ability to juggle is different, but students suggest you want some work but not so much work that you jeopardize your grades and your financial aid—and your sanity. You want to avoid too much debt, but you also want to avoid losing your financial aid because your grades dipped too low.

That said, there are many students who work full-time while going to school full time. Monty grew up in a Haitian family that put a high value on education so he knew that the break he took junior year couldn't be permanent. Turned out to be three years, but when he returned, he kept his full-time construction management day job and took all his classes at night. *"I was a twenty something guy living like a 45-year-old man. I got up, went to work, went to school, came home, studied, ate, slept, repeat. I had to register as early as I could to get the time slots I needed. It was pretty crazy, but I did it and I'm glad I did it."*

Look for work that fits your biological clock. If you like to study in the morning, get a night job in the campus café. If you study best at night, try to find a desk job at the gym in the mornings.

Rene regrets thinking she should not work part-time freshman year. *"I thought I wouldn't focus on school if I had a job, but when I started working junior year, I saw it wasn't a problem. Most of the jobs are used to having students, and there was flexibility around exams and stuff. I needed the money so I should have gone to work at least a few hours a week right away."*

Cara wanted to apply for a research job but decided she was unqualified, so she never applied. She doesn't want you to make the same mistake. *"Just apply for what you want and advocate for yourself."* Work is where she found her mentor. Or you can do it in reverse. If you have a mentor, talk with that person about finding the right part-time job for yourself and about how many hours make sense. Students who work often end up doing a better job of time management than those who don't.

Students who have financial aid packages are often eligible for work-study which means the federal government is going to cover part of your salary. That makes you a good deal for an employer, usually on-campus or a non-profit organization in the community. Pay attention to campus research opportunities. Working on a research project is a good way to link toward career opportunities after college. You may be assigned a campus job, but you might also go looking for places you want to work, places where you can try out an emerging interest. Visit the principal investigator; sell your curiosity, your commitment, and your work-study funds.

DEBT

Among the 60 students we interviewed, debt went from zero to $125,000 for the man who chose a private historically Black college as an undergrad, the online University of Phoenix for a master's degree while working and an online Ed.D. also while working. Because of his income, he could only secure loans after undergrad school.

Loan debt of twenty or thirty thousand dollars, often more, is not unusual among low income, First Generation students. Debt is a weight, and it can interfere with plans to get married, have kids, and buy a house. How people feel about it is all over the place:

"I left the military after seven years, and they paid for tuition and some housing, but I have $30,000 in loans we needed just to live. My wife has about $20,000. But $50,000 has bought us a whole new life, a bigger, richer, more interesting life. It's easily worth it."

"I wish my high school program hadn't pushed four-year colleges over the community college. Looking back, I regret not starting at the community college. I think I would have gotten as good an education, and I wouldn't be so in debt."

"I knew when I chose a private liberal arts college, I was taking an expensive option. Now my mom and I have about $60,000 in debt. But I would do it again. It was a terrific experience for me, and I value those years deeply."

"I wish, when I was taking out all those loans, I had thought more about what it was going to feel like later."

There is no right answer about what you should do. It is "right" however, that you know your options. It is right that you don't fall into a choice without being aware of the cost and the cost of other options. Students with an uninformed bias against the community college never considered it. Great students who assumed they could never afford an expensive private school never considered whether they could win a full scholarship. Students who were sure community college was the only affordable option never considered anything else.

Sometimes, a more expensive school, perhaps in another state, will offer a better aid package than less expensive public schools close to home. If you haven't made a decision about college, you are finishing at community college and need to move to a four-year school, or you are thinking about transferring, take a look at a website called MyinTuition[23] that can give you a quick and easy sense of what college costs would be for you. You may find that by leaving your city or even your state, you will be given a better financial aid package than if you stayed close by and chose the cheapest local school. *"I didn't want to go away,"* Sophia remembers, *"but I was offered better scholarship support by needing more money to live away than what I could get living at home. It was a better deal financially, and it turned out to be a better deal experientially."*

Every year, more states offer tuition-free options for low- and even middle-income families. Some states have free community college or tuition grants at state schools. If you don't live in one of these states, consider whether it would make any sense to move,

---

23 https://myintuition.org/quick-college-cost-estimator/

spend a year establishing residency and then take advantage of free tuition. Do you have family in one of these places? Unless you can live with family or friends, it will mean you have to pay for a place to live, find a job, and make new friends. There are dangers in taking that route. But know it's an option and think about whether it could work for you.

Look for companies that have tuition reimbursement policies. Maybe you find a job with a company that will help you with your college costs. That was the deal Eli fell into with a national construction company that he found both rewarding and satisfying. You can research these companies on the web.

Or what about going to college in another country? It is possible to go to the state university in Mexico for about $1,000/year and living costs are low. What you save with this strategy could finance a master's degree in the U.S. after college. Other countries also offer lower-cost options. One way to get a U.S. degree but save on tuition (but incur travel costs) is to work with your college to spend a year abroad in a college in a country with lower costs that collaborates with your school so your credits all transfer. This is obviously more complicated, but if the idea of living abroad appeals to you, do your homework. You could start with this site: **https://www.collegechoice.net/popular-international-universities-us-students/**.

As this book is being written, the Coronavirus has forced students into online classes. This has led to a general reassessment of online education. Online options have existed for some time, but Covid-19 is creating more opportunities for students to go to school online at lower financial costs. We don't yet have good data that look at whether this kind of college education lessens the ability to develop social, cultural and emotional capital. It certainly makes social interactions more difficult, but if you are debt adverse, you may want to explore these options.

MONEY MANAGEMENT

When we have just used hundreds of words to acknowledge how little money you may have, it may seem odd to now talk about money management, but several of the people we interviewed urged us to include this section. *"If you don't learn something about money management before you graduate, you are going to be in trouble,"* was a repeated warning. *"I am a terrific budgeter now that I'm working, but I wish I had learned how to manage my money better in college when the numbers were smaller. It took a lot of effort to know how to budget money once I had it,"* Cara says.

What do these First Gens think you need to learn?

■ Start saving. Even when money is very tight, start the habit of saving. Maybe it's only a dollar or so a week but open an account and put something in it every month or even every week. Make what you want to save the first thing you pay out from every paycheck. *"Sometimes, I would start to buy something, maybe a Starbucks coffee, and tell myself, 'No, if I can afford that, I can instead put the money in savings,' and I actually did it. Turns out it adds up over time, enough to buy an expensive textbook."*

■ Learn some effective budgeting tools. Jeep budgeted his money by putting it into envelopes for different kinds of expenses and finding Instagram accounts that talked about financial literacy. There are several free online tools to help you construct a budget. Look at Mint or Nerd Wallet. Learn to write down all your projected expenses and then track them against what you spend and figure out where your money is actually going. *"I used to get so stressed when I ran out of money between paychecks,* Prisha recalls. *"I needed clarity about where the money was going, and it helped me when I figured that out."*

Starr reflects:

 We were always poor, and I just assumed we would always be poor so there was no point thinking about money. Once I started to learn about money and budgeting, I got obsessed for a while with tracking every penny. It was painful in the short run, but now I have a much more realistic understanding of what things cost and how we spend it and where I can save it. And it made me learn to cook.

■ We all get caught up wanting stuff that feels important in the moment but after we have it, we don't care that much. Be sure you really will get lasting value from what you buy. How much is a phone upgrade worth or a bigger cable package or a team sweatshirt? Would it be better to work a few less hours and do without? On the other hand, you are allowed a treat now and then. A couple slices of pizza should not trigger a case of financial indigestion.

■ Don't discount second-hand buying. *"I found brand new blouses at Goodwill for very little money, and perfectly fine toddler jeans were $2.50,"* a married student with kids tells us.

- Look for alternatives to buying new textbooks. Check out these sources for buying or renting books:[24]

Chegg	*Valore*
eCampus	*AbeBooks*
Textbooks.com	*CampusBookRentals*
TextbookRush	*Alibris*
Amazon	

- Get creative. One undergraduate on full scholarship redeemed his meal plan his sophomore year and banked the refund. He scrounged his own meals for most of a semester and then used the refund money to cover the upfront costs of renting an apartment that was less costly than his dorm and food plan. Then he started investing through a program called Acorn which allows you to use your credit card to save small amounts and invest.

- When my children were little, we didn't have much money, but we had an extra bedroom. For several years, we had an undergrad who lived with us and traded free room and board for help with the kids and dinner in the evenings. Gigs like this are available if you go looking. Put up notices in supermarkets and grocery stores in high-end neighborhoods. Tell faculty and staff what you are looking for.

24 http://www.openculture.com/?campaign_id=9&emc=edit_NN_p_20200406&instance_id=17375&nl=morning-briefing&regi_id=36211091&section=whatElse&segment_id=23997&te=1&user_id=22e5e65700a89efebf2b3432cc6a0cdb (link to free text books, etc0

■ Henry couch-surfed for a semester so he could give up his full-time job and raise his GPA. He used the school gym as his private retreat. *"It's not a great way to live, but it isn't awful either, and it let me do what I needed to do. When I worked full-time, school got neglected."*

■ Begin to educate yourself about money management. Tanya says reading the Mr. Money Mustache blogs really helped her figure out how she wanted to think about money. Starr and her husband followed Dave Ramsey, the online financial advisor, to get a handle on their debts.

TAKE ACTION

If you have never tracked your expenditures, is now a good time to begin? Perhaps you would like to find an online tool, build a budget and track where your money goes and whether it is possible to start to save.

Money is an instrument that helps us secure what is important to us. Make a list of five things you value most. What role does money play in securing those things?

8

ACADEMICS

Since the whole purpose of going to college is academics, why wait until the eighth chapter to talk about it?

This wasn't the original plan. Back in the beginning, this was the first chapter. But in conversation after conversation, it became clear that so much of what makes school hard, what causes people to drop out, melt down or despair, is not the schoolwork. Worrying about money, feeling out of place, thinking you are not good enough or smart enough or the right color gets in the way of school. Despair, depression, shame, fear of asking—all this affects your ability to do schoolwork.

College is not the end. It's the beginning. You might come to college specifically to learn about engineering or computers, auto mechanics or art—but the BIG things, the key things, are learning how to learn and figuring out who you are and what helps you achieve your goals. You need to pass your classes, often at a level high enough to maintain scholarships, and you need to graduate owning information and skills on which you can build in the years ahead. But most of all, you need that foundation on which to keep learning and growing in the decades ahead of you. Everybody should have that. This book embraces a college education as a valuable asset worth working toward and wants to help you graduate, but you have to commit to do the hard work.

MAKE SURE YOU ARE
WHERE YOU WANT TO BE

Just to be sure that now is your time to take on college, go to Appendix I. Look at the questions-to-self. Ask yourself those questions and think about the answers to help you decide if you are ready to spend the time and money on college NOW.

College is not the only road to success, although more and more career paths today demand special preparation. You might find it as an apprentice, in a certificate program at a community college, or with your own hard work and on-the-job training. While this book is all about getting through college because college is a powerful way to create opportunities for yourself, it is important to acknowledge that it is not the only way to find success and well-being. You might want to read *How to Find Good Work Without a College Degree* which can be found on Amazon for less than $6.00 (I also authored this) and lays out alternative options.

Sometimes, it takes a while to get your head into the place that lets you do what you need to do for school. If you are not ready, school is not going to go away. Jorge dropped out his senior year of high school after a stint in jail for a non-violent mistake that likely would have been much less punitive for a kid whose family had some money. That experience stuck him in a rut, and he worked at low-paying jobs for a decade thinking his window for college had closed. With encouragement and information, he found his way to a community college to learn to be a lineman, work he is loving. His first semester at school, with a wife and two kids, he had a 3.6 GPA. The hard part was not the schoolwork but believing college was actually possible for him and daring to say he wanted to be there.

Talisa, the daughter of Laotian refugees, was part of an Upward Bound program in high school,

> . . . and in the program, we were told we should go to college. We wrote essays and took tests and filled out forms. I didn't understand any of it. I didn't really know why I was doing all of it. But I applied to college and was accepted at a satellite of the state university. I arrived clueless. I didn't know you were supposed to think about a career. I had no idea how to pick classes. I took out loans I didn't understand. On my first paper my teacher wrote, "You need to go to the writing center because this isn't college level work." I was traumatized. After that, I never went to class. I failed out at the end of freshman year.
>
> As a First Generation student, no one understands you. Your family doesn't know why you are going to college and can't help you. You don't know about mentors. If you are like me, you don't know about anything. But I knew deep down I needed to go to school, so the next year I enrolled in community college. I repeated my mistakes and flunked out again. I said, "I'll never be smart enough for college." I gave up. Well, I didn't really give up because I knew I had to figure things out. It took me four years, but I didn't want to spend my whole life living paycheck to paycheck. When I did go back to the community college, I got straight A's. Now I'm finishing up a Ph.D. in speech pathology.

Talisa, clearly, never lacked the ability to do college work, but at first, she hadn't yet convinced herself that was really where she wanted to be and deserved to be. To ride the ups and downs of anything difficult, it helps to be firmly focused on the end point.

If you are choosing college, be clear that there are many different kinds of colleges and different paths to completion. Don't be a sheep and follow what the people you know are doing because you don't know what else to do. You know how to read, so spend a little time on the Internet, in the library, in a bookstore researching what is going to be right for you. You know how to talk, so talk to anyone you think can help.

HIGH EXPECTATIONS.
LOW EXPECTATIONS.
CHALLENGES EVERYWHERE.

Worry doesn't know privilege. It is everywhere, and what we are seeing is that students—about seven percent of low-income First Generation students—who are highly talented academically and rewarded with scholarships to highly competitive private schools—find this privilege can have emotional costs. Elite schools may seek out First Generation students but be insensitive to the systemic challenges that are baked into the school culture. Looking back, one graduate recalls: "*When I understood the system wasn't built for people like me, I felt less critical of myself.*"

When First Generation students see that some difficulties are systemic, it can empower them to challenge systems that are outdated and hurtful but unseen by many. One gift First Generation students bring is the ability to help their institutions become aware of structural obstacles that create unfair and unhealthy barriers to success. This offers their institutions the opportunity to face them and grow as the students are asked to grow. "Not everything that is faced can be changed," cautioned James Baldwin, "but nothing can be changed until it is faced."

Anthony Abraham Jack is a First Gen student himself who went on to get a Ph.D. at Harvard and is now an assistant professor at the Harvard School of Education. He has written a helpful book, *The Privileged Poor. How Elite Colleges Are Failing Disadvantaged Students.* Jack identifies two kinds of lower-income high school graduates coming to elite colleges: One group he calls the Privileged Poor. These are kids who have already become familiar with the ways and customs of the rich. Perhaps, like Jack, they spent time in a private school or a public school that allowed them to interact with more affluent kids, or they had summer enrichments that exposed them to the kinds of academic and social opportunities that families with money provide their children. The second group he names the Doubly Disadvantaged.

"When they first set foot on an elite college campus, it looks, feels and functions like nothing they have experienced before," Jack explains. They experience acute culture shock. In a process of intense interviewing, Jack probes the experiences of both groups of students. He describes how unfamiliar they are with the rules and customs of their new world.

> Students who do not feel welcome at a college do not avail themselves of the many opportunities and resources that are available. Campus life is often more stressful for these students than for their peers, hampering their ability to focus on various tasks. They tend to underperform and to give up more easily. Students who delay integrating into their larger college community also have less access to social support from their peers and from college as a whole—support that proves crucial to success both in college and in the labor market upon graduation.[25]

25 *The Privileged Poor. How Elite Colleges Are Failing Disadvantaged Students.* Anthony Abraham Jack. P. 28

SQUEEZE THE BEST FROM WHEREVER YOU ARE

What these high achieving students had to learn about how to "do school" can be applied to students in all kinds of colleges—big, small, public, private. What kind of school you attend introduces interesting issues. Schools that are ranked high academically often are populated in large numbers by non-minority, affluent students. On one hand, it is a good idea to go to schools offering excellent academics and a chance to develop friendships with people highly likely to be successful in the future, schools that offer all kinds of resources and have high graduation rates. On the other hand, our interviewees who attended such schools—and value the rigor of their educations—found the hyper-competitive atmosphere and sense or privilege undermined their self-confidence.

Coral grew up in Texas and was one of those students.

> Freshman year was scary. Sometimes I would feel like I was the only Hispanic there and didn't belong. And I struggled academically. In terms of academics, I fell very far behind. I had to withdraw from my math class first semester. I was completely intimidated. But then I got a B+ the next semester.

After graduating debt-free from college, Coral came home to Texas and took out a loan to enroll in her local state university in order to raise her GPA for graduate school. *"It's so different when everybody is working and going to school and half the kids are Latino.* She was surprised at how at home she felt on this campus. *Going away taught me so much about how the system works. It was a huge learning experience, but it was hard."*

Stacy did not get as generous a financial aid package as Coral, but she had her heart set on going to a well-respected private college. She was an excellent student in high school, and she wanted to be seen by others as outstanding. She also wanted to remove herself from her insecure family life and *"make something new of myself."* She only looked at well-ranked private colleges, took the best offer and ended up with $75,000 in debt. *"Now, I realize how narrow my thinking was. I should have looked at a wider variety of choices and been more sensitive to cost. And yet, the education I got is serving me well."*

Prisha chose to leave Texas, with lots of good in-state options, for an expensive mid-sized private Jesuit college in the west.

I hardly had financial aid at the start and it made no sense for me to go there, but I was desperate to get as far from home as I could. When they accepted me early, I just decided I would go. I was just running away. But what I found was that I really needed a full-blown, four-year comprehensive immersion to help me fully form my personhood and find my passion. There is something special about being somewhere where you are fully encompassed in an experience . . . I may have more debt than with other choices, but I don't think I would have this good life I have now.

A report from the Brookings Institute, a widely respected research organization, finds that:

Going to college is not enough. A great deal hinges on the quality of the education being offered. First Generation, Black, and Hispanic students are getting a lower-quality education than their socially advantaged peers. Gaps in college quality reflect disparities in education in the preceding years, of course. But right now, if anything, the college years see those gaps widen even further—which puts the ideal of equal opportunity even further out of reach.[26]

What to make of that? If you are in a community college or a school that does not rank high on graduation and retention (the percent of freshmen who return the next year), it does not mean you cannot do well. It may take a different kind of effort. Some students find themselves in situations where their peers' behaviors reflect unexamined privilege. On the other hand, you may find you are facing an environment with unexamined low expectations. Don't be influenced by this.

Set your own course. Expect your teachers to teach you and take in the best your school has to offer. Every school has some ineffective teachers and some great ones, some indifferent administrators and some caring ones. Martha went to a community college because it was all she could afford and because she had not done well in high school. Valeria was undocumented and unable to get financial aid. Both were disappointed at first. They felt *"lesser"* and feared they would get an inferior education. Both came away feeling challenged. Valeria is grateful for the engaged and caring faculty members. Martha learned how to be a student and is now finishing up her credentials to teach English. Valeria's green card came through just as she was ready to transfer, and she found herself well prepared for flagship university academics. Roberto went to a community college because he was a distracted hellion in high school with undiagnosed ADHD and didn't get accepted anywhere else. Now, he feels truly lucky and advocates community college as a first step to higher education. With his master's degree

26 Brookings report. Jonathan Rothwell, 12/18/15

in counseling, he now works with disadvantaged young people and thinks many of them will thrive in community college.

Your quest is to find the good and use it well. If you show faculty that you have a hunger to learn, they are going to respond by wanting to feed it. Your interest and determination will stimulate the best in them. You just have to be unafraid to show it and not worry about whether you are smart enough. Being hungry to learn is incredibly smart, and it is enormously appealing to college teachers and administrators.

After talking this through with lots of people, here is the sum of their advice. **Wherever you are now, concentrate on getting the most that you can from it.** If you are in a community college with a serious interest in academics, consider working your way into an honors program and/or a mentorship program. Do as well as you can, and, if you wish to continue for a bachelor's degree, leverage the community college degree into continuing at the most highly ranked four-year school you find available to you. Don't assume you must stay in the same city for your last two years just because that is what most students do. If you are in a four-year school ranked in the lower half of schools, again, there will still be great teaching. Work hard and establish a stellar record. Consider a transfer as you learn how to function in college, or stay put and be the hungry student every teacher wants to help.

TAKE ACTION
What benefits are you gaining by attending the college where you are currently enrolled? If you still have a few more years of college, will this campus continue to be the best fit for you? If you have doubts, speak to an advisor or colleagues about transfer options.

HOLES IN YOUR HIGH SCHOOL EDUCATION

Many students, both at community colleges and four-year schools, are required to take remedial classes. National statistics report that about half of all First Generation college students start in community colleges and well over half of community college students in all income groups have been taking at least one remedial course in college, most often math. Four-year schools can also require remedial classes.

Recent research has shown that from a quarter to a third of students required to take a remedial class could have earned at least a B in a regular class. Happily, big changes are afoot.

Colleges are changing the way remediation is measured and the way academic deficiencies are addressed.[27] Some schools are offering intensive low-cost summer prep courses. Ohers have "co-requisite" classes which are credit granting but also provide remediation formerly addressed in non-credit classes. You can go forward while filling in the holes from the past.

The point is not to ignore your educational gaps. Houses built on shoddy foundations—maybe cheap cement or unstable soil—have trouble down the line. Don't build your education on a faulty foundation. Just get it right now, and it will always be yours. No matter how much you believe you cannot do it, others who were sure they also "could not do it," often found they could.

---

27 https://www.educationdive.com/news/how-colleges-are-reshaping-remedial-education/557120/; https://www.brookings.edu/research/evidence-based-reforms-in-college-remediation-are-gaining-steam-and-so-far-living-up-to-the-hype/

If your high school did not do right by you or you did not do right by high school, okay, that's the past. It does not define your future. But don't make the same mistake twice. Get a grip on basic math and English skills. Career opportunities in the future will build on this; most importantly, if you can learn to learn, if you can figure out how to get your mind around material that at first may seem difficult, you are laying the groundwork for your future success.

Math is the subject that is most likely to bedevil students. Don't fear math or run away from it.

> . . . math skills are increasingly important for getting good jobs these days—so believing you can't learn math is especially self-destructive. But we also believe that math is the area where America's "fallacy of inborn ability" is the most entrenched. Math is the great mental bogeyman of an unconfident America. If we can convince you that anyone can learn math, it should be a short step to convincing you that you can learn just about anything, if you work hard enough.[28]

Carol Dweck is a Stanford University professor who has done excellent work on the connection between mindset and success. What Dweck wants you to know is that what you may label a failure is not a permanent condition. It is a "not yet." Failing is not a signal that you lack ability, but rather an indicator that you need to get busy growing more of your brain capacity. Dweck has used brain imaging to show that when we give up, our brain fails to light up. When we decide we just need to push through,

28 https://qz.com/139453/theres-one-key-difference-between-kids-who-excel-at-math-and-those-who-dont/

our brain lights up and we start producing more brain cells. In short, we can make ourselves smarter by leaving our comfort zone and learning something that is difficult. One recent graduate, now headed to graduate school, told us, *"Part of my success may have come from having that 'it's not over yet. I just need to re-tool' mentality."*

To get a quick understanding of Dweck's powerful work, a short but good online article is footnoted—you can probably read it in seven to ten minutes—on the growth mindset.[29]

TACKLING CLASSES

A minority of students only have to deal with school. Many more are also juggling work, family, transportation, health and psychological challenges. Maybe you are even coping with love life problems. A recent report says that, as of 2017, 43% of all full time and 81% of part-time undergraduates were working while in college.[30] How can you get good grades and do all you need and want to do in the time you have?

It is possible. But we want to go back to that idea of learning how to learn. This is like doing warm-up exercises before you go out to play the game so you don't injure yourself. Take some time and give some effort to putting down a foundation for learning that is going to help you ever after, going forward. That's a promise!

Prisha recalls:

> I never saw school as something I could conquer. I never believed I could be a straight A student—until I could, until I figured out how to do it my way. I saw that I had to put more hours in if I really wanted to know something. It wasn't until my junior year, in a philosophy class that I "got it!" Oh my God, I never felt I could totally understand what was given to me, but once it happened, it was so exciting, and then I saw that when I "got it," I could apply it.

---

30 Education Dive, 2/40, Natalie Schwartz, https://www.educationdive.com/news/gen-z-takeover-could-online-colleges-gain-traction-with-young-students/575484/

First thing, find 12 minutes when you can listen to a video and completely concentrate. This short talk explains clearly how our brain works and what we need to do to retain information. Isn't that what school is about? You are presented with content and then examined to see how well you retain and understand it. And you want to know it longer than five minutes after a test.

So, listen to Will Schoder tell you how to do that. Just type the name *Will Schoder* and *How to Remember Everything* and you will be taken to his YouTube video.[31] We know you are going to think you have got it the first time but make yourself go back and listen again a day or two later. You will remember his outstanding advice much longer if you do this.

Then buy yourself two books that have come highly recommended from other students:

1. *Learning How to Learn* by Barbara Oakley and Terrence Sejnowski.

   This book is $16 in paperback. We recommend you get a paper copy so you can write in it and re-visit it. It is 219 pages of easy-to-read print. It is written for kids and teens and is not a difficult read, but the advice is pure gold.

   Right now, take a look at Barbara Oakley's Ted Talk footnoted below.[32] She is an expert in helping people who "can't do math" figure out how to do math just fine and her methods apply to all subjects. Find a print copy of the book as well. It's worth it.

---

31 https://www.youtube.com/watch?v=V-UvSKe8jW4&t=6s
32 https://www.youtube.com/watch?v=O96fE1E-rf8

It will tell you why sometimes letting your mind wander is an important part of the learning process, how to avoid "rut think," why having a poor memory can be a good thing, and how to stop procrastinating.

2. ***How to Become a Straight-A Student*** *Unconventional Strategies Real College Students Use to Score High While Studying Less* by Cal Newport. This book is $15 in paperback with lots of white space and fabulous strategies for dealing with your classwork. Those strategies come from 'A' students at the most difficult colleges in the country and can be applied by anyone anywhere.

   It explains how to learn more in less time, how to take smart notes, write good papers and have more free time while getting better grades.

Did we say: **Read these books**! There are other great books, but we are thinking that if we just suggest two that are not hard, not long, not filled with small print and are considered by thousands of students to be full of helpful advice, you might really read them. If you want to read more, see the footnote[33] for books that want to convince you it is a lie to think you were born dumb and doomed stay that way.

Now, how about some specific tools that can help you? Is time management a problem? Probably. Lots of students found the lack of structure in college unnerving, especially that first semester.

33 The Art of Learning, Josh Waitzken
    Moonwalking with Einstein, Joshua Foer
    The Talent Code, Daniel Cole
    Talent is Overrated, Geoff Colvin

Procrastination is undoubtedly the most popular sport on campus. Many students confess to wasting time worrying about how much they had to do—without really doing any of it. If, however, you have been making a consistent effort and are having more trouble than seems reasonable to you, check out the section on *Wacky Wiring* in Chapter 8, **Taking Care of Yourself.** It is possible you have an undiagnosed learned disorder that has nothing to do with ability and everything to do with physiology.

Read the syllabus. The syllabus is handed out at the beginning of the semester, and it tells you what will happen in the class, what the readings are, when tests will happen, and papers are due. It's the story of the class. From it, you can make notes in your calendar about what you will need to do when. **Having a schedule—and following it—is key to time management.**

Another key to doing well is making the most of class lectures. If you learn how to take notes well and use those notes effectively to take charge of the material, you will have a much easier time studying for exams. Try the Five R method for notetaking:

1. RECORD

2. REDUCE

3. RECITE

4. REFLECT

5. REVIEW

Consider looking up online the *Cornell Notetaking Method,* which is designed to help you through these five steps.[34]

Not sure how to tackle writing a good college paper? There is all kinds of advice online. See if this article cited in this footnote on a site called *The Shovel,* can help.[35] For more comprehensive help, you might check out Owl, Purdue University's writing center which is online and offers excellent advice and direction: **https:// owl.purdue.edu/site_map.html**

But interviewees' best advice is to take yourself over to your own campus writing center. Their job is to help you. Let them do their job. And if you give it a serious go and get back a poor grade and/ or critical comments, make an appointment with the professor during office hours and say, *"I need help learning how to do this better, please."* Or go before you start the paper. It is very normal for students who received only As and Bs in high school to find themselves with low grades at the start of college. It is not only you this happens to. It is a message that says, "Okay, time to up your game. Time to ask for help. Time to find out what the new expectations are."

The value of meeting with professors or teaching assistants extends way beyond writing papers. If you get lost in class early, chances are you can get more lost later. Lost is not good. But if you already knew this stuff, you would not need to take a class to learn. **Feeling lost is a message, like pain, saying *oops, something is wrong; can we fix it?*** Don't wait until it is too late to drop a class or fix your grade or find yourself hiding under your pillow. It is

34 http://lsc.cornell.edu/study-skills/cornell-note-taking-system/
35 https://howtostudyincollege.com/how-to-get-good-grades/how-to-write-a-college-paper/

dumb, more dumb, dumbest to pretend you can cope when you need help. Asking for help not only shows you are smart, it will, in fact, help you get smarter about whatever is driving you nuts.

TAKE ACTION

Do take time to listen to Will Schoder and How to Remember on YouTube.

If you feel lost in a course, take a minute to get clear about one thing you can do to help yourself. Check back over the advice you have been offered and see if you are avoiding a trouble spot.

STUDENTS' STRATEGIES FOR
GETTING BETTER GRADES

"I saw that I had to put more hours in if I really wanted to know something."

"Part of my success may have come from having that 'it's not over yet. I just need to re-tool' mentality."

"Once I learned to take classes because I wanted to learn the subject, it was a game-changer."

"I had no idea what kind of effort college required. If it hadn't been for the mentors from my high school program, I would have waited way too long to ask for help."

"I have found that staggering assignments and not procrastinating was very effective"

"If you are faced with a question you can't answer, maybe "What topic should I pick?" or "Where do I begin studying for this test?" and you just can't figure out an answer, then you need to ask a question that precedes it."

"While you are fresh, start with the hard stuff. Maybe you can't finish it all but tackle one piece. Each day figure out what you plan to accomplish for the day."

"One way to learn something well is to teach it to someone else."

"Be realistic about the time good schoolwork takes"

PICKING A MAJOR

Students talk about the pressure of picking a college major. Many, looking back, think they could have made a better choice for themselves. Turns out, in a national survey, 61% of college grads would change their major. While in school, 70% change their major at least once and more than half of those change it at least three times.[36]

There is "supposed to" and then there is "what is." Careful of "supposed to." That was Fernando's story. He was supposed to choose courses that would lead to a lucrative career, but they made him unhappy. Are you supposed to go to medical school but never enjoy your science classes? That was Anna who kept trying to make the wrong major feel right. Are you supposed to prepare for law school but find nothing about the classes interesting? Cecilia, who hated her political science major but thought it was what she should do, owns that one. Are you supposed to get a community college certificate in a trade, but secretly think you would make a great teacher? Or do you fear that aiming for an electrician's apprenticeship isn't prestigious enough although what you want is to be an electrician? There are many painful stories of students who came to school with a script about what they ought to do and, looking back, realize they needed a script that fit them better. *"Be patient, take it slow,"* cautions Tai, who thought he would never make it through college until he found the major he loved. *"You do not have to know what you want to*

36 https://www.nytimes.com/2017/11/03/education/edlife/choosing-a-college-major.html

do when you get to college. There is lots to sample, so do that before you lock in."

On the other hand, if you are coming to college specifically to improve your income and work opportunties, you may want to know going in what you want to do coming out, find the best place to learn it and be laser focused on your goal. If you are interested in a certificate program, do your exploring before you register so you put yourself in the right place from the start.

Different schools have different rules, but usually you do not have to declare a major until the end of sophomore year. Don't be in a hurry if you plan to be there for four years. It is fine to be undeclared for a while. Rene, wanting to feel she had a purpose, chose a creative writing major before she began school. Along the way, she began to second guess her choice but was afraid she would not graduate on time if she switched and didn't want to take on any more debt. But she never had a conversation with her advisor or found a complementary minor. She graduated, returned home, ended up working at Starbucks for several years, and now, four years out of school, finds herself floundering for a clear direction.

Advice about majors has an on-the-one-hand and on-the-other-hand quality. On the one hand, you want to find subjects that excite you and engage your mind. On the other hand, you don't want to add to your debt by delaying graduation. But you certainly don't want to end up with no good plan for employment.

What could have helped Rene was a vision for her working future with a Plan A and a Plan B. She would have benefitted from professional work opportunities during school. Finding summer work that offered experience and contacts related to her interests would certainly have been helpful. Maybe you can figure out how to get a taste of careers you are considering early on by volunteering. Ife launched her marketing career by volunteering to do the marketing for campus groups and graduated with a portfolio of work to show employers.

It was volunteering that helped Maria discover that she did not want to work as a floor nurse, but later, in another volunteer internship, found out how much she liked the fast pace of ER work. Jerrie found unexpected passion and emotional support as well by falling into a minor she never considered:

> I could never register on time because my parents were not availabe to fill out FAFSA, and I had all these money issues. By the time I registered junior year, all the cool polical science classes were filled. All that was left were these cross-listed classes in Jewish Studies. It was a Catholic school and no one wanted those, so there I was, the only Black girl in class. And I loved it. I ended up with Jewish Studies as my minor and it gave me free travel to Poland, Germany and Israel. Getting involved with holocaust rememberance helped me get through college. It put my life in perspective. My minor became everything.

Anna remembers what it felt like when she finally abandoned her bio major:

> I approached school with the goal of graduating, not thinking about what I wanted to do. Once I learned to take classes because I wanted to learn the subject, it was a game-changer. In the end, I still wasn't in the right major, but my advisor helped me find classes that interested me and would fit the requirements of my business program. We tilted it toward business psychology.

Ranesh had to resist parental pressure to focus on engineering or medicine. His parents didn't get why he would be a business major, but he knew himself well enough to know their choices were not right for him.

In this footnote are two good articles to check out if you are struggling with a decision about your major.[37] Remember the wise words interviewees offered earlier: Beware the "supposed to."

Here is one idea for how you can get a handle on your own "what is." Pick a handful of friends, people who know you well and whom you think have good judgment. Tell them you would like their help by coming to a Pick A Profession night. Ask each one to think about two things they think you could do well in the world. Go around the group twice and ask each person to tell what one is and why it makes sense. Then as a group, play with it. See if anything useful comes to you.

Another helpful thing to do is visit the campus career center and ask to do a career assessment. If we are really good at something, it is easy to think it really isn't anything special because it comes to us easily. Find out what you do well compared with other people. Find out what kind of work is suggested for people with your strengths. That's one clue to career and major choices. If you have your heart set on something that doesn't come easily, of course, forge on. Just know you will have to work a bit harder.

Freshman year is not too soon to go to the Career Center. You can go back when you are actually ready for help with a career. And you should. The Career Center may help you shadow a person

---

37 https://collegeinfogeek.com/how-to-choose-a-major/; https://www.nytimes.com/2017/11/03/education/edlife/choosing-a-college-major.html

139

doing work you think will interest you. Spending time with them can help you decide what really makes sense for you.

There is an aptitude test called The Johnson O'Connor which tells people how they score compared to others on various aptitudes. They have a huge sample, and what they have learned is that you do not have to have a high aptitude to do well in a profession, but if you naturally have aptitudes related to the work you choose, you are likely to be successful and find it less difficult. Taking the aptitude test in person and getting follow up counseling is costly, but check out their free online book[38] to understand the basic aptitudes and figure out some of this for yourself.

Another inventory that many find useful in thinking about career choices is the Myers Briggs Type Inventory. It will help you understand what characteristics related to work will be more satisfying for you. Within every field, there is work suited for all types. You can find a version of the inventory online, but many campus career planning offices offer this assessment, and you should definitely ask on your campus. Alternatively, you might ask if anyone in the psychology department is certified to administer the MBTI inventory for you.

You may just want to check off that 'pick major box', have a decision, and feel like you are working purposefully toward a goal. But think of it like a soccer game. If you get turned around and are running toward the wrong goal, it is not a victory.

Students in community college can face an especially challenging landscape. More colleges are moving toward letting students first

38 https://www.jocrf.org/aptitudes/book-understanding-your-aptitudes

identify a career framework and then work their way toward a specific field, but this does not exist everywhere. Many community colleges have a shortage of advisors and counselors. Less than half of community college students say that an advisor helped them to set academic goals and create a plan for achieving those goals. A Brookings Institute report raised this as a factor that gets in the way of graduation:

> We find that the typical student is overwhelmed by the many choices available, resulting in poor program or course selection decisions, which in turn cost time and money and lead many students to drop out in frustration . . . During initial advising sessions, there is typically not enough time for long-term planning, goal-setting, or a thorough orientation to college life and how to navigate from enrollment to completion.

So, what do you do? First, decide this will NOT be you. If you can find a program on your campus, whether it is a community college, a state school or a private school oriented toward First Generation students, go sign up immediately. To use our favorite word once again, ASK for help in learning how to pick a major and lay out your courses. If every class is not offered every semester, it helps to be thinking ahead. Ask upper classmen, ask work supervisors, ask faculty. You may get different answers. Put them all in your pocket and when your pocket is full, dump them on your desk and sort through what feels true for you.

Certain majors may be useful for admissions to graduate programs or to get your foot in the door for work, but once you have been out in the world for a few years, no one will care what your major was, and you don't need a school curriculum to determine what you learn. You get to keep learning all your life, in school or not. If you decide you made a mistake, okay. Figure out the next steps.

Stacey majored in Latin American studies but had many classes in the sociology department. Senior year, she decided she wanted a Ph.D. in sociology, and encouraging faculty helped her apply to the best departments in the country. But without more sociology background, her acceptances all came without scholarship support. She took a year out to re-group and found a master's degree program in Latin American studies that offered opportunities for sociology courses. This got her a full-ride scholarship at a major state university, and she anticipates sliding into the sociology doctoral program.

TAKE ACTION

Before you pick a major, try making a list of a handful of career areas that seem appealing to you, then work backwards and ask yourself what skills they would require. In order to get a bigger picture of all the kinds of work in the world, read the last chapter in this book and start asking all kinds of people about the work they do and how they got there. We pick majors from a small list. You want to pick a career from a much bigger list.

FIND HELP

You heard Rose's voice in the chapter about money. She is the young woman who finished in the top 10% of her high school class and then failed three of her four classes her first semester in college. Like so many First Generation students, Rose had no idea how to study for college or what was expected. She assumed she was supposed to know this and felt embarrassed to admit to anyone how overwhelmed she felt so she just drowned on her own.

Tanya, on the other hand, found herself at a small but demanding private college in New England, also struggling with college expectations. She marched herself into her professors' offices and said, *"I don't know how to study for a class like yours. Can you please teach me?"* And they did. For most of the semester, she met twice a week with one of her professors who coached her on how to study and explained what college-level expectations were.

Stacey grew up in a chaotic and distracted family with little stability. As a result, she relied on high school teachers to give her guidance and encouragement. When she got to a small liberal arts college where small classes were the norm, it was easy to continue to relate to her teachers:

> I made a point of getting to class early and just talking with the teacher. Just things like, "How was your weekend?" or "What you said last lecture about such and such was so interesting to me." It makes you known and you have a connection with them easily. I try to see my teachers as people, not authority figures and so they see me as a person, too. You don't have to have a problem to go meet

with a professor. You can just go to say, if you mean it, I liked that last lecture, and here's why. **"**

In interview after interview, we heard the same message, which is why it keeps getting repeated: You may be shy. You may be an introvert. You may feel uncomfortable asking others for help.

Get over it. Tell your teachers when you are lost. Use the resources of your school to teach you what you need to learn to manage the work. It isn't that you lack the intellectual chops.

Student after student talks of finding their early college academic experiences difficult: *"I really never had to work in high school. I had no idea what kind of effort college required. If it hadn't been for the mentors from my high school program, I would have waited way too long to ask for help."*

Here is one more voice with a good idea for how to find help while sitting at home:

" I couldn't have done well in my classes without using the tutors a lot, but sometimes it wasn't enough. I was too busy or they had too many people to help. So, I started using YouTube, especially for math. I could always find videos that explained what I was working on, and I would just watch it over and over until I understood it. **"**

When you listen to First Gen stories, it's clear that it is fear, lack of good study skills, inadequate school preparation, and/or low self confidence that gets in the way of academic success rather than brain power. Sometimes it's something as simple as thinking what worked in high school will work the same way for college. If you had to be a genius to get through college, we wouldn't have more than 80 million graduates today.

TAKE ACTION

If you have never been to chat with a professor, pick one now. Write down your opening lines. Maybe it's as straightforward as "I read a book about success in college that says it's a mistake not to talk with professors and told me to pick one I wanted to know. I picked you, but now I'm a little nervous . . ."

THE GREAT KILLER: OUT OF TIME

The path to doing mediocre work—or worse—is to run out of time. Avoid, postpone, daydream, shoot hoops, and then suddenly, the exam, the paper, the project is upon you. Here is what students say: "*When you are not sure how to begin, you put off beginning.*" The longer you put off beginning, the less time you have to do it right.

Consider an idea called The Previous Question. If you are faced with a question you can't answer, maybe "What topic should I pick?" or "Where do I begin studying for this test?" and you just can't figure out your answer, then you need to ask a question that precedes it. Maybe your questions are:

- *What's a good way to pick a paper topic?*
- *Who can give me some advice about this paper topic?*
- *What would actually interest me in all this?*

If you are faced with studying for an exam and you want to go eat doughnuts instead, ask yourself: What is it about this that is putting me off? Can I lay out a study plan? Is there a study group I could join? What scares me?

When you really try, seriously, to go forward and you keep finding a wall, it is time to go sideways. But you must go somewhere. As Cal Newport explains in his book, good students find there is plenty of time to get their work done and still have a personal life. The key is planning and organized study habits. You do not need an exceptional IQ to manage this. You do have to convince yourself that you can do this, and you want to do it. And then . . . well, do it!

A student from a highly competitive school says:

> I have found that staggering assignments and not procrastinating was very effective. I usually found myself well prepared for exams and having ample free time along with consistent seven-eight hours of sleep even, though I also had a campus job. Granted, I did not do much partying and most of my socializing was on the weekends through volunteering, dating, or dorm events.

You may be surprised to know that, on average, students who work do better in school than students who do not. They are forced to learn time management. But how much you work is a factor. You have to decide for yourself how much you really must have the extra income, how much you need to sleep and how much time you need to get a good education. The right equation is not the same for everybody.

Be realistic about the time good schoolwork takes. Often it is going to take longer than you think so don't under-estimate work. Better to over-estimate and have time to kill. My husband teases me because I always set my watch and car clock fast. It's because I know I tend to run late and this is protection. Aim to finish ahead of time so you have a cushion if needed.

FOUR YEARS OR
MORE YEARS

In the U.S. we talk about four-year colleges for a Bachelor of Arts or Science degree and two-year community colleges for an associate degree. The goal is to finish the first in four years and the second in two. Of course, not everyone is doing that. In fact, most college graduates are not doing that. It's common to take an extra year or even two. If you are worried about money and debt or if you have a scholarship that limits your time in school, you don't want to pay for extra semesters. And then there is the woman who wanted no debt. She spent ten years working toward her college degree and regrets none of it.

Part-time students, certainly, take longer. But if you are enrolled full-time, it's a good idea to finish "on time." It is expensive to spill over into another year. You are paying more tuition, more fees and more time you could apply elsewhere. Your scholarship may run out in two or four years. Students who arrive with college credits from AP classes or community college courses they took in high school can sometimes graduate even more quickly and save a semester or two of college costs.

To limit debt, figure out how to graduate in four years or less. It may mean staying with a major you decide was not your best choice, but it allows you to graduate on time. Figure out if you can pursue what interests you most in other ways than switching a major if the switch will add time you cannot afford. Explore all the course options for your major and see if there is a way to meet the requirements with classes that interest you more than what may be the traditional route.

From year one, make a chart with all your required courses and think about how you are going to meet the requirements semester by semester. Every class is not offered every semester so check and make sure the classes you need are going to be available when you are planning to take them. It may make sense to consider taking a class during the summer at a local community college to complete a requirement.

You may find yourself confused by all the requirements. Read the college catalogue. Go over what you understand with an advisor. Use your advisor, but double check for yourself. It's okay not to know all this stuff when you start. But it is costly to fail to learn it.

At the start of senior year, double check with your advisor to be sure you are on track to graduate on time. Follow that meeting with an e-note of thanks and brief summary of the conversation so that you have a record of this assurance. Starr was told she could do an online course to meet a major requirement only to find out when she completed her application to graduate that this course left her shy one credit. It ended up costing her $600 she didn't have in a summer session for one credit. She could not prove that an advisor approved her choice.

Students who are assigned to remedial classes can lose time there. Students who fail classes can be set back. Students who cannot get a space in a required class that their major demands can get derailed. Changing majors is probably the number one reason students end up spending more time in college.

If you want to apply to medical school, taking science courses helps. If you want to work in finance, you will need some classes that work with numbers. And yes, your major can help you get a job in fields related to that major—but there are other ways.

Internships, work assignments, class projects can be used to develop depth in a field of interest or personal recommendations to help you crack into a field unrelated to your major. Once you have a couple of years of work behind you, few will ever care what your major was.

MAKE LISTS

When you read Cal Newport's book, you find how highly successful students value lists. When we juggle all the things we need to do in our minds, it feels very heavy. Sometimes it feels impossible and leads to a kind of paralysis. Write it all down. Keep an up-to-date list of everything you need to do: school, work, and personal stuff. Maybe you have three columns. When you can see it all laid out, it is easier to set priorities. Don't put huge tasks down as one thing. Break it up into chunks so that you can accomplish one part of the whole and feel virtuous instead of feeling bad because you can't cross off the whole thing.

There can be a temptation to deal with the little, easy stuff first. You know, *"I'll just clean my desk and then my room and then I can start on my term paper."* While you are fresh, start with the hard stuff. Maybe you can't finish it all, but tackle one piece. Each day, figure out what you plan to accomplish for the day. Make a schedule and write it down because it is easier, we heard again and again, to follow through on what is written down.

THE READING LIST

Students everywhere can feel overwhelmed by the amount of assigned and suggested reading on each class syllabus. You never get to the end of all the suggested reading. That means you have to prioritize what you must read.

But there's more. Decide when and where you are going to read it. If your roommates are in and out or play loud music, don't read on your bed. Find quiet corners around the campus where you can tuck in and have an intense and focused half an hour before you take a break. Figure out what times of day you are best able to concentrate and plan to do your hardest work then. We are going to hype Cal Newport's book *How to Become A Straight A Student* again because there is so much helpful information there about managing all the reading that we are not going to repeat here.

TAKE ACTION
Get that Newport book.

STUDY GROUPS

One way to learn something well is to teach it to someone else. In order to explain material clearly, you have to understand it yourself. In some study groups, each person is responsible for summarizing a section of the material. You are forced to focus hard on one part and then you have "experts" in the room with you who can explain other parts with which you might want help. Not always, but mostly, these groups tend to be very supportive of all members as long as they are trying and doing their part. If there is no group, or you suspect you are either invisible to your peers or just excluded, try to you can find a study-buddy with whom you can work. Maybe you have to be a bit pushy and ask to participate since solid research finds students in study groups perform better on average than students who work only alone.

A good time to join a group is at the start of the semester. One student talked about meeting people when she explored club memberships, then encountering them in class and linking with them to study. Other students talked about feeling they would hold a group back or feeling invisible when groups formed. Shyness can get in your way here, and if you can push it aside long enough to speak up and ask to be part of a group, excellent. Lynda, who describes herself as a shy introvert, was busy working full time and did not join groups. But she discovered that by getting to class ten minutes early and hanging out in the hall with classmates or waiting in the classroom gave her a way to meet her peers which sometimes led her to say, *"Hey, want to meet for a cup of coffee and talk about the upcoming exam?*

If you feel you are demanding more of a study group than you are contributing, say so. Tell them you know that teaching something to you will help them retain the information, but that you feel awkward about your contributions. Ask the group what it thinks you should do. That's hard because you will feel vulnerable, but it is also brave.

If you are not sure how best to organize a student group, see the short article in this footnote below.[39]

---

39 https://entertolearn.byu.edu/how-organize-and-conduct-effective-study-groups

CHEATING AND PLAGIARIZING

This whole section can be summed with one word: Don't! If we were to add a second word it would be Really! Don't!

There is an external and an internal reason. The external reason not to cheat is that if you are caught, you may be expelled. We think that's fair.

And the internal reason goes back to the start of this chapter. The key thing college is teaching you is how to learn. Not doing the work cheats you. We can't tell you what kind of person you want to be in the world. We can't even say that cheaters never get rewarded. We can't crawl inside their brains and see if they find happiness in cheating, but we doubt there is a deluxe corner of heaven that caters to cheaters.

TAKE ACTION

In reading through the sections in this chapter, did anything click with you . . . make you think, "I need to pay attention to this especially?"

Go back to that section and make a plan for doing something differently.

COLLEGE IN THE AGE OF THE CORONAVIRUS

This page is a late insertion. As this book goes to press in July 2020, there is no clarity about what will happen for college students in the 2020-21 school year. It looks like many classes will be offered online. That adds another challenge to the academic experience.

Many of the recommendations that interviewees offer you in this book come with the expectation that you will be on campus. Here are some suggestions for adapting to learning online.

1. **Create good mental and physical space**, a place to work online that limits distractions, is comfortable and has room for stuff—book, pads, pencils, etc. If you don't have this kind of space at home, can you find a place that feels safe nearby? A library, a closed business whose owner you know, the home of a relative who is out working . . .?

2. **Block social media** for chunks of time while you are listening to lecture or focusing on school work. There are apps that will save you from continual distraction. Use one.

3. **Ask!** is the most important piece of advice from successful First-Gens. Don't give up on asking remotely. Use email, for sure, but don't hesitate to pick up the phone and ask for a few minutes to talk or leave a message asking for a call back. It is the job of college faculty and

staff to help students, so don't feel reluctant. Working to build connections is all the more important when you are learning remotely.

4. **Talk.** Because it is harder for people to develop a clear sense of you remotely, help them be aware of your interest and curiosity by speaking up, asking questions, and participating in online chats.

5. **Connect.** What you can't do in person, you must do at a distance. Connect with classmates and faculty. A good follow up is to send a note saying, "*I found what you said in class . . . and I would welcome a chance to talk about this a little more. Can we schedule a phone conversation?*" Have a thank you template you can adapt and use regularly. Join a virtual study group. You benefit from having others know you and you knowing them.

6. **Move.** It can get tiring staring at a screen all day. Stretch. Schedule walks. One student says he propped his computer up on Amazon boxes so he can sometimes go to class standing up.

7. **Have a routine.** Think of school as you would a job. Schedule your work hours. Plan your breaks. Align working with your internal clock and do the hardest work when you are at your best. You don't skip work shifts; don't skip lectures or discussions.

8. **Looking good in Zoom.** Have good lighting in your room. Make eye contact by looking at the camera, not the picture. Consider investing in a microphone. But, make sure you are on mute unless wanting to be heard. Take off your sleep clothes. And don't make negative comments in chat. If you want to complain, do it offline. If you want to get more comfortable with zoom, they have posted a video just for students: https://www.youtube.com/watch?v=wbnyQwsVbiY

MORE IDEAS FOR COPING WITH COVID 19

So much of everyday life has been cancelled while we recover from Covid 19. For many of us, the world feels LESS. Here are ideas for how to find a little MORE.

1. **Trade Room and Board for Services:** If living at home is difficult, it may be possible to trade some help with children or an older person who could use a hand in exchange for room and board. Perhaps faculty or staff at your college might be interested. Start with an email to the Dean of the Faculty. Call or send a note to the head of houses of worship. (Reach out to those in affluent parts of the city on the hunch that more income might correlate with bigger houses and more extra rooms.) Reach out to student and professional groups. Then agree to a trial period to make sure you will be comfortable.

2. **Find a quiet place to study:** Do you have family or friends who work while you need to study and might let you use their home? Is there a nearby restaurant only doing take out that would let you hole up at a corner table near a plug? Is there an unused classroom in your place or worship?

3. **Reduce your debt:** If you must take all your classes online, is it worth considering switching to a school that offers lower costs for you? Look at these and other online resources:

https://www.thoughtco.com/how-to-earn-an-online-degree-by-examination-1098143

https://www.thesimpledollar.com/loans/student/affordable-online-colleges/

4. **Develop a regular exercise program:** You are stuck at home. Life has been derailed. Easy to fall into a slump. All the more important to exercise for mind and body. Join a dance class, find an online routine, lift weights, take up jogging or jump roping or high stepping or anything else that gets you moving. Put it on your schedule and be faithful. Would it help to set it up as a competition with friends?

5. **Work at making contacts:** What might happen spontaneously now has to be planned. Use the time you aren't commuting or socializing to connect with faculty and staff and with alums doing work that interests you.

Be intentional about making contacts. How about reaching out by email, phone, zoom to one new person every week. Use the alumni directory and/or contact student services. Connect with all your teachers. Here is some help in making the connection: **https://www. scribendi.com/academy/articles/how_to_email_a_ professor.en.html**

6. **Graduate faster:** For many of us, it seems like everything has slowed down. The days creep along. What if you use the slowness to speed up. You can't socialize. You are not commuting. You may be working less. So, go to school full speed ahead and graduate a year or more earlier than you planned. Push yourself to double down on school and get to graduation quicker than you planned.

7. **Learn how to be a top student:** So many people who were interviewed started out as poor students and, along the way, discovered school work was not as hard as it had previously seemed. What if you use this time to learn how to be a top student? Begin with the two books recommended in the *Tackling Classes* section of Chapter 8, Academics. Read the rest of the advice in that chapter and pick one or two courses and practice it. If you know you have an academic gap, find free online classes that let you fill in what you need to learn and build the future on a strong knowledge foundation.

8. **Teach yourself a new skill:** The internet is its own global university. There is so much to learn for free, stuff you might never consider in a busier, more demanding life. Learn to play the guitar, make something, cook something, see or listen to something completely new. Pick a place you have always wanted to visit and go there online. Explore some musical niche or curiosity. It's all there with no tuition . . .

9. **Become politically active:** If you think there are things in the world you think we need to change, join with others who want the same sorts of change. Educate yourself on the issues and the ways in which you can help. This first semester leads into November elections. Help the elect people who want to see the kinds of policy you think are good for the country.

10. **Expand your reading and listening habits:** Do you get most of your information from Facebook or a few select sites? Go broader. Decide to read an online newspaper or some news magazine articles. Listen to some new podcasts. Tune in to public radio or BBC. Try websites focused on first generation college students and on community activity groups with which you identify. Read books that are not assigned. Your school library can help you access all this online. Find out what you don't know that you don't know.

11. **Learn a new word every day.** Go here: **https://www. merriam-webster.com/word-of-the-day/calendar** and sign up to get a word and its definition in your inbox every day.

12. **Travel:** Never been to an art museum or the zoo or Venice Italy? Go now with a virtual tour. **https://www. goodhousekeeping.com/life/travel/a31784720/best-virtual-tours/** This is just one list of suggestions. Always wanted to go to . . . Paris? Deep sea diving? Nascar races? It is all there for you to explore with the time you are not spending on campus with friends.

13. **Learn a new language:** You don't need a language department or even a language class to learn a new language. Here is some advice on how best to do this: **https://www.babbel.com/en/magazine/10-tips-from-an-expert** and here are places to learn for free: **https://www.inc.com/larry-kim/9-places-to-learn-a-new-language-online-for-fre.html**

14. **Find pleasures:** In the middle of loss, find small pleasures. Some days are just difficult days. Want to try to develop the habit of finding one bit of pleasure every day?

And, finally, consider an intentional conversation with the people you live with. Sit down together and talk about what is going on and how you feel about it. Figure out what can work best for each of you.

9

TAKE CARE OF YOURSELF

Maybe you will live in four different houses, love three different people and change your clothes size from small to large to small again in your lifetime. You will, however, only ever get to live in one body. Since it is going to be with you forever, it makes sense to keep it in good working order.

As a young person, you may not spend much time thinking about how to take care of this body, but tons of good research show that if you neglect nutrition, sleep and mindfulness, you perform less well. Since you want to get the best out of college, it's worth spending a few hundred words to focus on how to help that happen.

EAT, SLEEP, EXERCISE. REPEAT.

Maybe this will sound counterintuitive and rub against what you have believed to be true. However, this section is not based on interviews but on substantial data.

Medical research finds that eating well and sleeping sufficiently allows us to function better, much better. Exercise helps both mental health and learning. You may really feel you don't have time to sleep seven or eight hours a night or always eat healthy meals instead of junk food with your busy schedule. The goal here is to try to convince you this is mostly a mistake.

Adequate sleep, healthy food, and a regular dose of exercise make people more efficient. It takes less time to accomplish our goals and our performance is better. People who study all night do not out-perform people who take an exam well-rested. People who substitute coffee and corn chips for a real meal because they feel short of time do not function as well as people who are eating healthy fruits and vegetables. Taking twenty minutes to exercise can tune up your brain so that it remembers with greater accuracy.

Here is what Dr. Matthew Walker, one of the world's leading experts on sleep research, tells us:

> Humans need more than seven hours of sleep each night to maintain cognitive performance. After ten days of just seven hours of sleep, the brain is dysfunctional as it would be after going without sleep for twenty-four hours. Three full nights of recovery sleep (i.e. more nights than a weekend)

are insufficient to restore performance back to normal levels after a week of short sleeping. Finally, the human mind cannot accurately sense how sleep-deprived it is when sleep-deprived. (*Why We Sleep*, p.140)

You may have long functioned on less sleep and think you are different. Dr. Walker is well aware of such people. In response, he quotes one of his research colleagues, Dr. Thomas Rother at the Henry Ford Hospital in Detroit: "The number of people who can survive on five hours of sleep or less without any impairment, expressed as a percent of the population and rounded to a whole number, is zero." They are a fraction of one percent of the population. You are not likely to be one of them. That you may have been living this way does not allow you to appreciate what it would be like if you lived on more sleep. Nor can you see now the long-range damage you are doing to your body.

Insufficient sleep plays havoc with our emotions, aids depression, disrupts our concentration, and impairs our judgment. Walker's book *Why We Sleep* is a fascinating read if you need to be convinced of the role of sleep in doing well in school and every other facet of your life. If you want just a taste of Walker without reading the entire book, spend twenty minutes watching his TED talk. You can find it by searching for Matt Walker, *Sleep is Your Superpower*.[40]

If you, as many interviewees, believe sleeping seven hours/night is just not feasible, we invite you to give it a try for just one week and note whether you seem to function any differently. If sleeping

---

40 https://www.ted.com/talks/matt_walker_sleep_is_your_superpower/transcript?language=en

more allowed you to study less and be more effective, would Walker be convincing?

Poor nutrition has similar effects. Years ago, a nutritionist named Adele Davis told us, "You are what you eat." Turns out, it's true.

Unfortunately, like an expensive car, your brain can be damaged if you ingest too much low-grade fuel. Multiple studies find a correlation between a diet high in refined sugars and impaired brain function—and even a worsening of symptoms of mood disorders, such as depression. It makes sense. If your brain doesn't get good-quality nutrition, there are negative consequences. What's interesting is that for many years, the medical field did not fully acknowledge the connection between mood and food.[41]

If the medical field missed it, college students certainly miss it. You are busy, you are short on cash, your sources for quick easy food are usually loaded with carbs and sugars. You are depressed by your workload, and it never occurs to you that the pizza, beer and cookies you are eating to feel better contribute to depression.

Eat regular meals. You can skip breakfast, contrary to what your grandmother may have insisted, but when you eat, you need to go big on the vegetables, get some decent protein, skip the carbs and desserts. Trade soda for water. Find healthy snacks. A doughnut is not a healthy snack. Keep a jar of peanut better in your room and spread it on some vegetable. Keep an apple on your desk. Think of good nutrition as a calming, legal, over the counter drug you can use every day. Drink water and stay hydrated.

41 https://www.health.harvard.edu/blog/nutritional-psychiatry-your-brain-on-food-2015
    11168626

Move your body. "Movement . . . increases energy, reduces stress, and calms the mind and body. Research shows that exercise may stimulate the production of brain chemicals norepinephrine and dopamine, which energize and elevate mood."[42] You probably already know this but knowing something and making it a practice are different activities. Can you figure out how to put exercise into your schedule?

You can multi-task with movement. Coral, who describes herself as shy and introverted, hardly made any friends freshman year. Sophomore year she wound up her courage and joined a dance group. The exercise felt great, but so did the friendships she found. Jorge loves basketball, and that drew him to pick-up games in the school gym where he really met the guys he had seen in his classes. Rose never had time to exercise between her full-time job and classes and constant stress. It was she who ended up hospitalized. Exercising is a way to meet people and make new friends.

If being involved with a group is just too hard to schedule, take advantage of the school physical fitness facilities. Usually, they are open long hours, and you might be able to squeeze in a workout in bits of time between classes that aren't so useful for studying.

At the least, consider walking. Head to the most serene place on your campus, turn off your phone, take some deep breaths, and take a walk practicing mindfulness.

42 https://www.moundsparkacademy.org/news/2019/01/03/the-relationship-between-movement-and-the-brain

TAKE ACTION

For one week, how about tracking your sleep? Write down how much you sleep each day. Do you want to track your exercise as well? Once you have some data, you can decide if you want more or less sleep, more or less exercise. Measuring our behaviors helps us manage them.

WACKY WIRING

One smart professor asked us to include a section on neurological disorders that make it difficult for students to concentrate, interact or complete schoolwork. "So many of my First Generation students have undiagnosed learning disorders but hesitate to talk about them for fear they will seem less capable," she explained.

Sometimes school difficulties that you believe are your own fault are really the result of wacky wiring in your body. Without understanding what is happening, it is both easy to beat up on yourself and miss out on learning how to manage what is a medical issue.

Students who fidget, are easily distracted, make impulsive decisions, find it hard to complete tasks and are told they are careless or forgetful may have Attention Deficit Disorder (ADD). A version of ADD adds hyperactivity (ADHD) to the mix. This causes us to burst with energy, talk forcefully, and have trouble focusing. This says nothing about our intellectual abilities but makes it harder to complete schoolwork, as this young man attests:

I used to think I was just a screw up because my teachers were always scolding me or sending me out of the room. My parents never took us to the doctor unless we were really sick. It wasn't until I had health benefits in college that I found out my difficulties were medical not emotional. It was such a huge relief.

Between five and ten percent of Americans are thought to have some ADD issues. Frequently, people do not discover there is a medical cause for their struggles until they are adults. Sometimes, it only happens when their own children are diagnosed.

Another wiring problem is called dyslexia. This is a learning disorder that affects the ability to read, spell, write, and speak. Kids who have it are often smart and hardworking, but they have trouble connecting the letters they see to the sounds those letters make. It is more prevalent in boys than girls. It cannot be cured, but it can be managed. Dyslexia runs in my husband's family. Our intellectually-able son was frustrated as a child because reading and writing were so painful. The computer helped with writing and today he reads avidly, but almost entirely audio books. About three percent of American students are thought to have dyslexia. It is more common in males than females.

A third wiring disorder is autism. This is a developmental disorder characterized by difficulties with social interaction and communication, and by restricted and repetitive behavior. This is a spectrum disorder, meaning it can show up in different ways and different degrees. About one to two percent of young people have some form of autism.

There are other medical issues that can get in the way of your learning. You might need glasses or a hearing aid or, as discussed in Chapter 5, **The Importance of Emotional Well-Being**, have wiring that affects your moods. The point of this section is to help you understand that you did not cause these problems, and it is possible, once you understand what is making schoolwork more difficult than you think it should be, to find help. But first you have to have a diagnosis so if you have access to medical care, bring the difficulties that are plaguing you to the attention of someone trained to figure out what's going on.

One good way to access resources for yourself is to work through a campus office that might have a title like Resource Disability Office, Disability Coordinator or something similar.

SEXUAL ASSAULT

Trauma is bad for our health, and sexual assault is traumatic. In sixty interviews, only one person spoke of being sexually assaulted in college. But if the national statistics are right, there should be several more in our sample who experienced unwanted sexual contact.

The statistics are all over the place. One says that 13% of undergrads experience non-consensual sexual contact. Another, the Rape, Abuse & Incest National Network, tells us that among undergraduate students, 23.1% of females and 5.4% of males experience rape or sexual assault through physical force, violence, or incapacitation. Many assaults, as the one in the telephone interview, are never reported. Whatever the true number, it is too high.

During orientation, pay attention to the safety information you will be given. Figure out what you will do if you are ever in a situation where you feel unsafe. Make sure you know where you can go if there is an emergency.

Sexual assault is a complicated issue, both in discussing prevention and what actions should follow unwanted sexual activity. But what is clear and not complicated is that being assaulted by someone you clearly ask to stop or who used drugs to affect your decision-making is not cause for wondering what you did wrong. It is simply wrong that this happened to you.

If you have experienced an assault, the **National Sexual Assault Hotline can offer you confidential support. If you call 800-656. HOPE (4673)**, the promise is that you will be connected with a trained staff member from a sexual assault service provider in your area.

There is so much more to say about this traumatic subject, and interviewees who reviewed the manuscript before publication felt writing only these few paragraphs was insufficient. But it is the enormity and complexity of the topic and the lack of information from interviewees about lived experiences that result in brevity.

The subject is too important to ignore, too prevalent to avoid, yet I am not able to address it with sufficient knowledge. Rather than fail readers with inadequate information about how to protect themselves and what to do if assaulted, please go to this website:

https://collegestats.org/resources/sexual-assault-prevention/.

Here you will find data on the prevalence of sexual assault, the different kinds of assaults, ways to protect yourself and ways to respond if you or a friend has been assaulted. You will also find additional resources.

MINDFULNESS AND MEDITATION

Are you wondering: What is mindfulness?

Practitioners call it our superpower, a free, legal, access-anywhere power to give us calm and better health. The end goal of mindfulness is to reduce suffering. That happens when we begin to understand that we need not believe everything we think.

Our thoughts come at us whether we want them or not: *I don't belong here . . . I'm going to fail . . . I'm not smart enough . . . I'll never manage all I have to do . . . Life is impossible . . . Love is an illusion . . . I hate everyone . . . What is wrong with me . . . I'm invincible . . . Worry is useless . . .* They come every few seconds, like weather. Mindfulness doesn't ask us to stop those thoughts, argue with them, or accept them. It asks us just to be curious about them. To allow them to pass through us while we direct our brains to focus on the moment, on what our bodies are feeling, where our breath is going.

Mindfulness is awareness, and awareness comes by focusing on breath, taking it in, watching it, releasing it. While we are busy breathing and paying attention to breathing, our thoughts can come and go. Come they will, but if we don't engage with them, they will also go. What traps our thoughts, especially our negative thoughts, is the judgment we bring to them. If we receive them, notice them, and don't have any judgment about them, they move on.

Instead of acting on feelings, mindfulness encourages us to *feel* the feeling and think about whether it really is how we want to

174

feel. When we practice mindfulness, we are asked to sense only the present moment rather than rehashing the past or imagining the future. Are your shoulders tense? Relax them. Shake out your torso. Stretch your arms. Breathe deeply. Look around you and see what there is to see. And then breathe again . . . and again.

The purpose of mindfulness and meditation is not to relax you, but a more relaxed state is often the result. The purpose is to ease the pain we impose upon ourselves when we criticize what happened in the past or project our fears for the future.

If mindful meditation as described here doesn't feel like you, consider mini-time outs. For just ten minutes, turn off you phone, find a place you find comforting and hum a favorite song and recall a happy experience. Or keep your phone on, turn off the alerts and find music you love. Take a walk or stretch out and give yourself a ten-minute vacation. Stretch out on the grass and spend five minutes doing deep breathing. When you feel the most stressed, the most overwhelmed and you think you will never have time to do all that's waiting for you, just then, counter-intuitively, is a good time for that mini time out. The whole 'to do' list will still be there, but there is a chance it will be easier for you to tackle.

Mindfulness and meditation are mirror-like reflections of each other: mindfulness supports and enriches meditation, while meditation nurtures and expands mindfulness. Where mindfulness can be applied to any situation throughout the day, meditation is usually practiced for a specific amount of time. Mindfulness is the awareness of "some-thing," while meditation is the awareness of "no-thing."

THE DIFFERENCE BETWEEN MINDFULNESS AND MEDITATION

From *Mindfulness and Meditation* by Ed and Deb Shapiro

*"Mindfulness is the awareness that arises when we non-judgmentally pay attention in the present moment. It cultivates access to core aspects of our own minds and bodies that our very sanity depends on," says Jon Kabat-Zinn, from **The Unexpected Power of Mindfulness Meditation**. "Mindfulness, which includes tenderness and kindness toward ourselves, restores dimensions of our being. These have never actually been missing, just that we have been missing them, we have been absorbed elsewhere. When your mind clarifies and opens, your heart also clarifies and opens."*

Mindfulness also releases 'happy' chemicals in the brain; it lowers blood pressure, improves digestion, and relaxes tension around pain. It is simple to practice and wonderful in effect. Not a bad deal when all that is needed is to pay attention, which sounds like something we should all be doing but often forget. When we do pay attention, then change becomes possible.

Einstein said that we can't solve our problems from the level of thinking that we were at when we created them," writes Marianne Williamson. "A different level of thinking doesn't mean just a different emphasis in our thinking, or a more loving kind of thinking. It means what he said: a different level of thinking, and, to me, that is what meditation is. Meditation changes us, as it returns us to our right mind."

BITCH, GROAN, AND
BE GRATEFUL

Sometimes, we just need to bitch and moan. Something happens and it feels unfair. Or we make a mistake and the bitter taste lingers in our mouth. Our family or friends or bosses get on our nerves. It happens. No interviewee has told us to say, "Don't complain."

Go ahead, complain. Get it off your chest. But have a time limit for how long you can do this, and then tell yourself, "DONE." Now you get to poke at it and think about if there is a lesson you can take from it; like, can you protect yourself from having the same experience again? Ask yourself, "Did I have any part in how this went bad?" Eduardo insists that paying attention to his mistakes gave him some of his best life lessons. Then give it up to the universe and move on.

To balance the time you moan and groan, maybe you want to end the day—or start the day—with a gratitude list. Pick three things every day for which you are grateful. Big things like "I'm grateful I got a B in calculus" certainly count. But little things like "My roommate left me a Hershey Bar on my pillow" or "My mom sent me an unexpected 20 dollars" count too. Something that made you laugh, a small kindness you received, a beautiful flower seen on the walk to class—all these can go on a gratitude list.

TAKE ACTION
Right now, how about starting a gratitude list?
Can you list five things?

LISTEN TO THE SURGEON GENERAL AND OTHER WISE PEOPLE

✔ WEAR YOUR BIKE HELMET.

✔ BUCKLE YOUR SEAT BELT.

✔ DON'T SMOKE.

✔ DON'T DO DRUGS.

✔ DON'T GET DRUNK. (HAVING FUN AT COLLEGE DOES NOT REQUIRE DRUNKENNESS.) AND CERTAINLY, DON'T DRIVE DRUNK OR LET FRIENDS DRIVE DRUNK.

✔ DON'T HEAR YES WHEN YOUR PARTNER IS SAYING NO.

✔ IF YOU HAVE CONSENSUAL SEXUAL INTERCOURSE, USE PROTECTION.

✔ FIND A WAY TO CONNECT WITH OTHERS AND LOOK FOR FRIENDSHIPS.

✔ BRUSH YOUR TEETH.

✔ DO YOUR LAUNDRY.

✔ SMILE OFTEN. JUST SMILING IS PROVEN TO MAKE YOU FEEL BETTER.

TAKE ACTION
Go do your laundry. Smile.

THINKING
AHEAD TO AFTER
COLLEGE

After reading an early draft of this book, a recent college graduate emailed back:

> Navigating college as a First Gen college student is very hard. It's also hard navigating a career post-college graduation. There could be a "What Next?" section. For example, my sister and I always talk about how hard it is to pursue graduate school, plus gain career opportunities, plus look for jobs after college because a lot of it is about connection. Perhaps, there could be a little guide (but that could be a whole book too).

Other interviews pointed in the same direction: *"After graduation, no one tells you what's ahead, how challenging it is, how hard it is to find a job."*

That email brought Fernando's conversation back into focus. He talked about how some of his First Gen classmates seemed to be unemployed or underemployed because they had not understood how to position themselves for life after college. He, too, had struggled with finding a satisfying job.

Okay, it could be a whole book. Will you settle for a chapter?

START EARLY

First up, don't wait until the semester before you graduate to think about getting a job. Of course, you already have a full plate, but this isn't another research paper. It's an awareness, a curiosity about what people do for work that you keep in your pocket to pull out when you have a chance to be curious. You don't need to come to college knowing your major. One of the joys of the college experience is finding out about fields and ideas and activities you didn't know existed. You do that formally, in classes. We urge you to do it informally as well. This is not so much academic research as encouragement to be curious.

Especially if you attend a research university, look for faculty engaged in research that interests you and talk with them about the possibility of working for them. If you are a work study student, you bring a salary advantage with you to the employer. And being involved in professional research brings a work advantage to you. This is a chance to start building specific skills that can lead to work after college.

BE CONSTANTLY CURIOUS

Be on the lookout for work other people are doing that makes you feel like you might want to do that, too. Work on asking all sorts of people about work. It's an easy way to start a conversation. Ask your professors what their parents or their spouses or their adult children do. Ask the people you work with. Ask all the parents of your roommates and friends. This is just casual stuff—"Hey, I'm trying to learn about the world of work and how people end up in the careers they have. Do you have any good stories about that? What do the people you care about do?" When you get a reply that causes a ding in your brain, probe more. If you are really interested in knowing more about a career, ask for an informational interview which is a chance to chat informally about what the person does, how they got there and what they recommend to you.

Prisha is now working in fundraising and community development for a public affairs non-profit, a job she had no idea existed or would interest her in college.

> I spent a lot of time worrying about picking a major. When I first came to college, my vision of what career opportunities there were in the world was narrow. I didn't know what existed, and I worried that if I chose sociology, for example, I wouldn't be employable.
>
> Now I would tell others that your major doesn't define your career. Just find something that you want to learn about. Extracurriculars can help open career doors. But look at the GPAs for various majors. If you are thinking about grad school, some majors have, in general, lower GPAs which could make you less competitive.

Even if you think you know what you want to do, say, law or medicine or marketing, there are dozens of branches you can follow. If you have some direction, it makes it easier to know where to job hunt later.

There are thousands of different careers. Want to scan a career menu for ideas? Try this, where career options are grouped by category.

https://www.thebalancecareers.com/
different-types-of-jobs-a-z-list-2059643

And here is a really easy way to be curious without speaking to a soul. There is a great program called Roadtrip Nation that an early reader suggested might make sense for this chapter. Does it ever. Roadtrip Nation puts young people in a van and lets them drive around the country interviewing people about their work. There is no cost for the participants who are selected from applications, but they have to be willing to have their trip filmed. Then Roadtrip Nation puts the videos up on their website. To see all of them, there is a fee, but there is lots of stuff there free. It's interesting and inspirational.

Maybe you want to start with the hour-long video of three community college students unsure of what their career direction is who spend three weeks interviewing successful people who once attended community college, starting with the Chancellor of the California Community College System.[43] Jim Lehrer, a famous journalist and community college graduate, tells the students,

43 https://roadtripnation.com/roadtrip/community-college

"Make sure the life you lead matters to others because then it will matter to you." Since 60% of First Gen students say giving back to the community is important for them, this aligns perfectly. Another leader coaches: "It doesn't matter where you start. It matters that you start."

It is possible that your college career center can provide you with access to the entire Roadtrip Nation site. Ask.

NETWORKING IS KEY TO CAREER DEVELOPMENT

Eduardo prides himself on his skills as a strategic thinker, so he was surprised, midway through college, to discover that he was not strategizing for his future at a high enough level:

> Junior year, I suddenly realized I had not been playing the game as it should be played. All I knew how to do was read and write, and I needed a bigger resume. So, I canceled a chance to go to New Zealand for a semester because I realized I should sacrifice the semester towards networking and contacts, and I dedicated myself to networking. I was still doing what I knew how to do, but I didn't realize things got kicked up a notch. I didn't have social capital, so I didn't see at what level I needed to play the game.

He made an aggressive effort to become more visible on his campus with activities that could introduce him to people in his field of international diplomacy and college alums with clout in the world. *"I never went to a speech without making sure to meet and chat with the speaker afterwards."* He now has a contact list that satisfies him, and as well, a better understanding of what he wants from graduate school.

The **Networking Adds to Your Net Worth** section in Chapter 4 talks about the importance of contacts. That is such a bloodless word. How about relationships, friendships, mentor connections, wise advisors, and supportive adults? This links directly with the most repeated advice in this Guide: ASK. Ask for a conversation. Ask for information. Ask for a relationship. Don't ask by saying,

"Can we have a relationship?" Ask by actions, by showing your interest, offering your assistance, being appreciative. It is nice to have people interested in you, so be interested in others. Everyone will not have the time or inclination to connect, but many will, especially people with a connection to your college.

Looking back, Stanley thinks he should have worked a bit less and taken internships to explore the world. But he has an alternative

HOW TO START A NETWORKING CONVERSATION

■ Use your college alumni base to identify people doing work that interests you. Write or call, explain that you share a college connection and ask for a twenty minute conversation to learn about their work and how they got there.

■ Identify people you respect that may have helpful wisdom for you. Say to them, "You seem like such a wise and grounded person (or a passionate and committed person or successful and happy person . . . you choose . . .) that I would love it if you could find a half hour for us to talk about finding a career direction. I'm feeling so unsure."

■ Write an article for the school newspaper or a paper for a class and use that as the reason for requesting interviews with people who interest you.

■ Identify professionals connected to your college— doctors, lawyers, construction managers, architects, photographers—and ask to meet and talk.

suggestion: *"Learn how to network. I finally learned how to do informational interviews, and you can use your school alumni network to connect with people in fields that interest you. People like to help."*

In today's environment, résumés are submitted online and connectivity is also online. LinkedIn and Twitter are great vehicles for finding people whose work interests you. You also can join professional associations related to your interests. Most professional associations permit student members. Some have campus-based chapters.

Tyrone is a sophomore aerospace engineering major and is already feeling the stress of career planning.

It's always about who you know. The more networking, the better. I joined the campus chapter of the National Society of Black Engineers, and that's been great. I'm going to try to get on the board. For First Gens, race-based professional groups are really helpful. They can give you pertinent advice.

Alena had a chemical engineering degree and a 3.9 GPA—and couldn't find a job after graduation. Hear her story of how a seemingly unrelated connection led to the ideal job:

After graduation I was very depressed because I couldn't find a job. Finally, I called work agencies and started working as a temp secretary at an aerospace company. I was very unhappy. One of the secretaries saw how unhappy I was but also saw I was competent and worked hard. She had a friend in HR at a silicone company and they were looking for a chemical engineer, and she connected us. They asked me to come for an interview. It was seven hours meeting with different people. Two days later they hired me. It took me two years to get that job. I have been there two and a half years now, and I love it.

I now see I was not putting enough emphasis on my résumé. I didn't write cover letters. After school, I was tired and just wanted a break. And then, when I was ready to work, I just thought I was good enough and should be noticed. I didn't know how to do it better.

After graduation, no one tells you what's ahead, how challenging it is, how hard it is to find a job. I had three internships in college, but two were doing research on campus.

I did go to the career center, but it wasn't helpful. They never told me about practice interviews until after I was out of school, and by then I just didn't go. ⟋⟋

GET TO KNOW THE CAREER OFFICE

The career office is not just for seniors. Make friends with someone who works there. Be clear that you are looking for a long-term relationship that will help you land a good job when you graduate. Here are the services most career offices can provide to students, and it's not a bad idea to use all of them:

- **SELF-ASSESSMENT TOOLS.**
  These can help you get a clearer fix on what types of work you might enjoy.

- **INTERNSHIP PLACEMENTS.**
  Find out what internships are available and the best way for you to apply. You can start looking for internships your freshman year. Be flexible and open to all sorts of options.

- **RÉSUMÉ WRITING.**
  You career office is likely to offer résumé writing workshops and, perhaps, one-on-one critiques. You can write you first résumé early in your college career and use it for internship and part-time work applications and then add to it as you go on.

- **PRACTICE INTERVIEWS.**
  Mohad had a great academic record and some good internships in finance. He would be invited to interviews, but it never resulted in a job offer. He was so fixed on proving to interviewers that he was smart, that he neglected to develop any sort of personal connection in the interview.

If you are invited to interview, the company has already decided you might have the capabilities to do the job on offer. But do they like you? Are you someone people want to work with day in and day out? Are you interested in others and willing to learn or are you just wrapped up in yourself? Mohad is a nice guy and a good learner. He was just so nervous; he couldn't relax and be himself until he had a bit of job coaching. A great offer soon followed.

■ **ALUMNI CONTACTS.**
The Career Office should be able to connect you with alumni who are doing work that interests you. Call them. Meet them. Maybe shadow them for a day. Ask their advice. Many college alumni organizations have LinkedIn pages. Join the group.

■ **WORKSHOPS.**
It is likely the career office will run workshops or seminars from time to time. Sign up and go. See what you can learn that is useful to you.

■ **ROADTRIP NATION.**
The Roadtrip Nation website has scores of videos of successful people talking about what they do and how they got there. Many require a site subscription, but many schools can give you free access. The videos are delightful and waiting for you to explore.

TAKE ACTION

If you have never visited the career office, pick out one thing you could do there and go online now to make an appointment.

HOW DO YOU FOLLOW YOUR PASSION, IF YOU DON'T KNOW WHAT IT IS?

Common career advice is to follow your passion, but as Jorge asked, *"What happens when you don't have a passion?"* Don't panic if you feel passionless. Instead, start looking for "tasting opportunities"—chances to sample various kinds of work. Here are five ways to get those tastes:

1. VOLUNTEER
Use volunteering as a way to explore career options, make contacts and get connections for references.

2. WORK-STUDY
If you qualify for a work study job through the financial aid office, look around the campus and pick a place that interests you. You can take what's on offer or you can figure out what attracts you and go personally to see if they have a work-study slot you can fill. Because work-study salaries are subsidized by the government, it is a good deal for employers so go "hire" yourself an employer.

3. INTERNSHIPS
Actively look for internships. If you start freshman year, you will have a good chance of experiencing a couple of internships. Maybe you will have to work at a night or weekend job to afford taking an internship, but it can be a good financial decision down the line.

4. PART-TIME JOB

Find a part-time job in the community where you will get exposure to the world of professional work. As with on-campus jobs, be aggressive in asking for what you want to *taste*.

5. INFORMATIONAL INTERVIEWS

Simply said, this is just a conversation in which you ask someone: Tell me what being an X involves? How did you get here and how do you recommend I might get there? What do you really enjoy about this work and what is the challenge?

If you click with the person, you might ask if you can call again or shadow them or email for advice when you need it.

Here is some simple career math:

Ideas minus action = zero.

You don't need to focus on the top of the mountain if you can't set a big goal now, but it is a good idea to focus on a next step.

RECOGNIZE THE IMPORTANCE OF SUMMER EXPERIENCES

Students who are able to get some experience in an area that interests them have an advantage over students who don't. For many First Gens this is complicated by the need to make money in the summer and, perhaps as well, live rent-free at home. Try to figure out how you can land an internship that will be a stepping-stone after college. Observe what happened to Alena, above. She did have internships but two of them were doing mostly solitary research for professors on campus that did not lead to real-world connections. Her one corporate internship didn't click and her confidence took a hit. Now, her current employer thinks she is terrific.

Some professions weigh summer experiences heavily. Applicants to medical school benefit from medicine or science related college work. The finance industry frequently hires people who have interned with them as students. Architecture, design, music, theater are more examples of professional areas where people often get a start before graduation. If you don't have this, it does not mean you need to give up. Rather, this is encouragement to get a head start if you can.

Choose your summer experiences in the same way you choose your courses. If you have to live at home, be assertive about looking for internships in your own community. Don't wait until May to do that. Start calling, writing, connecting in January or February or even the summer before you are ready. **You know more people in your community than you might think. All the** people in your church, your parents' employers, your neighbors are potential sources of contacts.

TAKE ACTION

Imagine if you had no constraints. What kind of summer experience would you want? Then consider sharing that picture with others who might help you figure out how to have it or something close.

AND THEN THERE IS COVID-19

Writing this chapter in the middle of a world shutdown with a pandemic makes it harder to tell college students facing graduation what they should do. Our interviewees didn't yet have wisdom on this so we're turning to someone who has been out of school for a bit, but lived through two downturns when she needed a job.

Her comment is in response to a question put to her by David Abel, the editor of the *LA Planning Report,* and has relevance beyond her own career area:

Lastly Sara, what sage advice could you offer the students from schools of planning, engineering, and design in the class of 2020, who had anticipated six months ago that they'd be coming into a booming economy but instead now encounter a cratering economy?

I'm a really good person to ask because I cleverly managed to graduate in, not one, but two financial crises. I graduated from Stanford in 2002, during the dot-com crash, and from business school in 2010, when we were just coming out of the mortgage crisis. Obviously, broadening your search is very good, and getting any experience in real estate is important.

I think a lot of people—especially who do what I do—want to rush out and do impact right now, but unless you understand real estate fundamentals, you're not going to get there. If you happen to have extra time, this is the time to learn the fundamentals of whatever business it is. If you are going into real estate, now's the time to do some online coursework on what a cap rate is and how it works, or what a capital stack is and what it means, because too many people are going into this industry not knowing.

It's the same thing with impact. If it isn't your world, but you are getting into development, now is the time to learn, understand, and network. The thing that helped me through both of my crises was having a strong network. People are very active in social media; now's the time to follow others on LinkedIn and Twitter that you find interesting and engage them in conversation.

There's also a whole lot of online learning that's happening right now. You and I were very lucky that VerdeXchange had its conference before this all happened, but there's a whole lot of conferences that are going online. The important thing is not to just be a passive recipient of knowledge. That's helpful, but the key is figuring out how to use these to network. If there was an interesting speaker, reach out to them, see if they have some time to talk with you.

Understand the fundamentals and building your network are definitely the two things that I would be doing, but also looking to see who the winners are and being strategic. There are winners here who can't seem to hire fast enough. It's not a great time to go into retail sustainability, but it's a great time for healthcare, so going toward where the growth markets are.

NOW IS NOT ALWAYS

In my past, I ran a leadership development program for undergraduates at Rice University. At the urging of the women students, I organized a career day for women in the program. During that day, we had a panel, usually eight to ten women in different career areas that their students requested. I asked our guests to introduce themselves, tell us about their college major, what they did after college and what they were doing now.

Very few of those panelists, year after year, were doing what they thought they would do in college. Life happens. You probably know the quip, "We plan, God laughs." That isn't to say plans are folly. Plans, goals, dreams, desires, ideas, passions, hopes— all good. So is flexibility, patience, and determination. Mostly nothing turns out to be irrelevant.

Way back at the beginning of this book, we talked about how to measure success. But come graduation, many students—and parents—want only to measure success by the job you have and the salary it will pay. Jerrie was distraught to find out that after college, she was making the same $15/hour she made at Burger King as a student. It took her three more years to get to $25/hour and then, a few years later she doubled that. *"I didn't know upward mobility was about who you know."*

There is an ugly truth we need to tell you. Wage discrimination still exists. People of color are frequently paid less than their equally qualified peers. This needs to be addressed legislatively and culturally, but what you may be able to do for yourself is negotiate. Find out by using online tools and conversation, learn

HANDBOOK FOR FIRST GENERATION COLLEGE STUDENTS

what the salary norms are and advocate for yourself. Find alums from your school who work in the same industry and ask for their advice.

Life has this odd way of fitting the pieces together in that crazy quilt that is each person. So if you can't make something happen now, don't just give up. Do something. Learn something, volunteer somewhere, take an interim job, consider a related field. Consider an unrelated field. We can't know we want to do something if we don't know that something even exists. There are so many opportunities for you in the world. It can be a royal pain trying to open a door for yourself, but hang in there. Optimism and determination are excellent keys for getting those doors open.

TAKE ACTION

Write down three things you want to do this semester that can help you move forward after college. Commit to yourself a date by which you will do each one.

APPENDICES

APPENDIX I

EIGHT QUESTIONS TO HELP YOU DECIDE IF COLLEGE IS FOR YOU NOW

Most readers of this book will have already decided on college, but if you are unsure, try these questions.

1. Am I going to college because I don't know what else to do? Am I ready?

Somewhere around half of students start college directly following high school. However, the median age for First Generation students is 24. About a third of First Gens are over the age of 30, and 44% are married with dependents.[44]

If you don't feel ready for more school, if you really have no appetite or aspiration that college will fill, it might not make sense to take on the cost of college yet. Don't decide college is not for you. How about if you decide college is not for you now or not for you yet? Give yourself a year or three to answer three questions:

- *What do I think I want in life and do I think I can get there without more education?*
- *If I need more education, is college the right way to get it?*
- *Do I like the path I am on and can I see where it will lead?*

Have you considered a technical certification, often available at your community college or an apprenticeship program?[45]

---

44 https://whattobecome.com/blog/first-generation-college-student-statistics/
45 You might want to look at *How to Find Good Work Without a College Degree*. You can find it on Amazon as a paperback, e-book or audio book.

2. Have I gotten any advice from people who focus on college selection, and have I done any research myself?

High school counselors can be responsible for advising hundreds of students. They are most likely to focus on those who are assertive in asking for help, those who are outstanding, and those at risk for trouble. It is easy for you to get lost in the crowd. And sometimes, counselors have their own biases about who should go where without appreciating just what all your own interests and options could be.

There are, however, resources outside your school. Find one. Find more than one. Ask in the counseling office if your high school is connected to a program aimed at helping students enroll in college. There are national, regional, state and local programs and some are just within your school district. Go looking. Dozens of First Generation students spoke about how important it was for them to find a program before college and/or while in college.

Make contacts. Find teachers or employers or people at your church who understand the college decision process and ask them to talk with you. Get to know the librarian at your local library. Explain that you might not be able to follow their advice, but you are eager to learn all you can before deciding for yourself. **People really want to help you if you are open and curious, so if you are inclined not to seek out help, can you get over it?**

Half of all college populations in the country now are First Generation students. **Colleges need and want you.** There is a growing effort, all over the country in all kinds of schools, to help you be successful and graduate.

When you are in college, link up with a support program on your campus.

3. Am I college material?

As this book is being written, there are about 20 million students in the U.S. in college. Around five million attend private schools and nearly 15 million are enrolled in public colleges and universities. There are 4,000 two-year and four-year institutions. **Odds are good that there is a place that fits your needs**.

If you got reasonable grades in high school or you didn't get such good grades because it all seemed too easy and you got bored, yes, you are college material. But getting bad grades does not mean college is not for you. The key to answering this question *is being clear about what you want and how much you are willing to work for it.*

College comes in different flavors. What is right for you might be a four-year degree in philosophy from a small, demanding liberal arts college, a good business or biology program at the local state university, a degree from a culinary institute, a fine arts degree in painting or music, or a community college associates degree or certificate in a technical skill.

A better question is: **What kind of training would allow me to work in ways that interest me**? Everybody can learn and grow. Finding the best place for you to do that is the goal.

4. Am I an outstanding student with high grades and good test scores?

If the answer to this question is yes, you are part of a select group that the colleges are looking for, but you have to help them find you and be open to considering options that might have not yet crossed your mind. If you are offered a full scholarship including tuition and room and board, would you consider leaving your city and your state and going away? Would you be willing to take a free trip to consider the possibility?

Selective colleges across the country want to diversify their student bodies, believing that's part of a good education. Some of them, you never heard of. Go looking for them because they are looking for you. It is a wise strategy to compare financial aid packages from different kinds of schools in different kinds of places.

There are good benefits that a first-rate school can offer you—and there are difficulties to consider as well. Only 7% of First Gen students go to private colleges. There are many stories in this book about the gifts and the difficulties students in this group found, and you can decide what might make sense for you.

5. **What are the Pros and Cons of Starting at a Community College?**

Half of all First Generation students begin in community college. Community colleges are convenient, open to all, and less expensive than other schools. A bit over one third of all First Generation students are required to take remedial classes when they begin college, and the majority of those students are in the community college system. The community college is geared to getting students ready for college work with remedial classes because it admits all high school (and GED) graduates. However, the way remedial classes are being offered is changing and many schools now have opportunities in something called co-requisite classes that help you learn what you missed and still move forward and get college credit. Check this out if you are headed to a community college.

If you can possibly prepare yourself in English and math, the subjects on which admissions tests focus, while in high school or even after high school, do it! It's worth the effort because otherwise you may end up paying for the remedial classes but earning no credits toward college graduation.

The community colleges, in general, offer all kinds of tutoring and workshops to help students. If you are serious about learning, you can find the help you need. Other schools can also offer help, but it is always available at the community college level. Community college teachers focus especially on teaching and are usually good at understanding their students' issues. Students there speak with great gratitude about the tutoring centers and how helpful they are: *"I lived in the tutoring office my freshman year. I came from Albania and I didn't understand anything, but they helped me with everything. I am forever grateful."*

There are rewards, but also challenges, to attending a community college, and you want to know them up-front. Graduation levels have been low, but they are increasing each year as community colleges discover more effective ways to serve their students. It used to be that only 13% of students finished in two years, often because they must first complete remedial classes. Now, the completion rates are approaching 60% in six years.[46] The slower graduation rates can be explained, in part, by having a population that is usually working while going to school and often raising a family. Lack of money can cause people to take time-outs. So many graduates speak to the determination and resilience of many First Gen students in community colleges.

46 Education Dive 4/48/20

But it also puts you in an environment where completing a college degree in four or five years is not the norm, and the culture is not always helping to push and focus you. While schools work hard to create a campus environment that promotes conversation out of class, many students have only time to attend classes and then leave. The social side of college is harder to experience, and that part has great value too. Finally, because there is such wide variation in the academic ability of students, you may find many classes are less demanding than at schools with more selective admissions criteria. You may have to work harder to get an excellent education if you want that.

When comparing the cost of your community college with, say, a local four-year state school, of course, look at tuition but also the charges for fees and supplies. Look at how much it will cost if you want to take more than 12 credits in a semester. And consider what kinds of financial aid are available. Talk to students and alums and get a take on the campus culture. Knowing all this, you can decide what is the best value for you.

Another option that is slowly emerging and gaining in popularity is online degrees, especially those that are offered as an employee benefit. Starbucks was one of the leaders in offering their staff the option of free tuition at Arizona State University Online. Uber now has a tuition program, restaurants in Philadelphia have a program, UPS provides some tuition. You can Google "companies that offer tuition benefits" to see what is currently available. Be very wary of for-profit schools. Do lots of research before moving in that direction.

The coronavirus in the spring of 2020 forced campus closures and accelerated distance learning. It is likely that by the time you are reading this, the online options will have expanded and, perhaps, costs will have fallen. Many students argue that having face-to-face classes and being on the campus in person is valuable, but if the only way you can find to access a college education is online and you want a college education, do it.

6. What if I make a mistake?

Mistakes are allowed. Mistakes can be corrected. When you choose a college, you are only choosing for one year or, worst case, one semester. If you pick a college that does not work for you, you can transfer. If you fail a course, you can take it again. If you have a meltdown, you will find help and glue yourself back together.

Don't beat up on yourself. Just learn from the mistake and then, like the rest of us, you can go on and figure out how to make another mistake—and learn from that. However, the purpose of this book is to help you learn something from what others have learned so maybe you can make fewer mistakes. That's good, isn't it?

7. What are retention and graduation rates, and why do I care about them?

Retention is the percentage of students who start as freshmen and return to the school for a second year. High retention rates are one good indicator of student satisfaction and success. If you Google the name of any school and add retention rate to your search, you can easily find this number.

The most selective schools, those that take 25% or less of all applicants, have the highest retention rates, usually in the mid-nineties. On the other end are the least selective schools, those with open admission policies, and their retention rate, on average is in the sixties. You can get an excellent, satisfying education at these schools. But you are likely to find that more students around you will struggle academically and that the campus culture will accept dropping out more easily than at schools with very high retention rates.

It can be easier to stay on track and graduate on time if you are in an environment where that is the norm, or you are aware of the challenges and prepare to deal with them. "There is strong evidence that low income and Black students do better at more selective colleges compared to students with similar academic credentials who attend less selective colleges."[47]

To give you a sense of your options, 237 colleges and universities have retention rates of 80% or higher. More than 100 have retention rates of 90% or higher.[48] You might want to consider whether any of these schools could work for you.

To give you some perspective, let's use the city of Houston TX as an example. Rice University, a highly selective private school, has a 97% retention rate. The University of Houston, a public university ranked #185 in the nation has a retention rate of 85%. Its downtown campus (UHD) has lower admissions standards and a retention rate of 66%. Texas Southern University, which

47 https://www.brookings.edu/blog/up-front/2020/03/02/college-for-people-like-me-how-majority-black-campuses-boost-social-mobility/
48 https://www.usnews.com/best-colleges/rankings/national-universities/freshmen-least-most-likely-return

is the fifth largest historically Black college in the country, has a retention rate of 57%. The Houston Community College, with open admissions, has a 46% retention rate. All college and universities in Texas average a 68% retention rate. Every one of these schools has a lot of satisfied, successful students, but the culture is different at each one.

Graduation rates tell you what percentage of students who begin as freshmen, graduate and how long, on average, it takes them. When you attend a school with high on-time graduation rates, you increase your own chances of graduating. Again, you can graduate and graduate well-educated anywhere. But when students do not have parents who can help based on their own experiences, and sometimes don't value a college education, putting themselves in environments with a strong focus on the value of the degree is useful.

We talk about retention and graduation rates so you will know what challenges you might need to address. You know that people who drive have car accidents. Still, you drive. You just know that you must be careful and attentive; if you don't, you up your odds for a crash. The goal here is to help you get through the college experience with no crashes, and if you do crash, have the conviction that you can get the machine back in working order.

8. Am I assuming I can't afford college without researching all the financial aid options?

Financial aid is complicated. The young man who founded the First Gen group at Ohio State University told us it is the subject that most interests members of his group—and these are people who are already in college. There are many different ways of financing a college education. Many of our interviewees regret not looking more deeply into financial aid options and not understanding the long-term impact of various loan options.

If you want to go to college but think it is just not something you can afford, investigate more fully. Consider all the different ways there are to give yourself an education. A good way to begin to understand financial aid is to visit the official government website, **www.studentaid.gov**.This site will introduce you to FAFSA, the main financial aid form that every student seeking aid will fill out. Another good resource is **www.scholarships.com**. The FAFSA form, by innumerable accounts, is a pain—but a necessary pain. You want to figure this out and make sure you use it to your best advantage.

APPENDIX II

THOUGHTS ON CHOOSING A COLLEGE

Yes, **Crack the Code** is for students who have already decided to go to college or are currently in college. BUT . . . educators who work in high school college success programs asked for information on choosing colleges.

There is so much to say, but fortunately good books on college selection and admission already exist. You can find them in your college guidance office, the school library, the public library, online, and in bookstores.

Here are two of the many that we like:

A Starter Guide for Clueless Students and Their Parents
by Jake Seeger.

$10.23 with tax, in paperback from Amazon.

*The College Solution: A Guide for Everyone Looking
for the Right School at the Right Price (2nd Edition)*
by Lynn O'Shaughnessy.

$18.71 with tax, in paperback from Amazon.

You are about to spend years of your time and thousands of your dollars on college. Don't buy blind. READ the Seeger book and if you want more detailed information look at the O'Shaughnessy book. Maybe you could read it with a group of friends and discuss it. If you are not yet a high school senior, try to connect with a college prep program.

The interviewees in this book did have some things to say about choosing a college. There is talk about the benefits of staying home or going away, about parental expectations at odds with yours, the value of diversity, and the pros and cons of community college compared to four-year schools. Check out the section on *Debt* in the **Money** Chapter (7.) Take a look as well at the *Make Sure You Are Where You Want to Be* and *Squeeze the Best from Wherever You Are* sections in the Academics Chapter (8). Use the free MyInTuition cost calculator **https://myintuition.org/quick-college-cost-estimator/** to get an idea of what different kinds of schools might cost you. This won't give you a total cost because there are expenses beyond room, board, tuition, and books, but it will get you close.

If you are not yet a senior in high school, think about how you can shorten the time you need to spend in college to graduate by taking Advanced Placement classes and scoring high enough on the exams for college credit. Consider taking community college courses in place of some high school courses if your school board allows it and earning college credits before high school. Consider taking online college classes that could count for credit in the summer. Saving a semester or a year of tuition is significant, especially when money is tight.

Before we focus on picking a school, a word about funding your education, one more time. The FAFSA form, the required federal application for loans and grants, is, by everyone's reporting, a serious pain. And you will need your parents to cooperate in filling it out. Twenty percent of students who are eligible for federal grants never apply. Do not be one of them. The second book recommended above is full of good information about college funding and sources of help.

Half of all college freshmen go to a school not more than two hours from home. Only 14% attend schools within a 500-mile radius. But if you look more broadly, you may find a school that suits you especially well at a better price. These suggestions below are intended to help you become deeply curious about what might await you:

1. **ASK**: Follow the advice of college students in Chapter 3 and ASK. Ask all kinds of people who know you for their ideas about colleges to consider. Ask your college counselor, but also ask teachers you like. Ask neighbors you respect. Ask people at work or your place of worship. Ask serious students in your school. Ask graduates of your school now in college.

2. **BE IMAGINATIVE:** What if you went to college in another country? What if you moved to a state that offered free tuition for residents? What if you looked at schools that let you earn the price of tuition by working while at school? Here are some less than traditional ways to think about college:

   - The eight colleges in the Work College Consortium integrate work and school and allow you to work your way through college with no debt.

     https://workcolleges.org/

   - Would it work to establish residency in a state that offers free tuition options?

     https://www.nerdwallet.com/blog/loans/student-loans/
     tuition-free-college/

   - It's a challenge to go to school in another country, but if you speak another language, you might consider it.

https://studentloanhero.com/
featured/6-countries-with-free-college-for-americans/

■ Some students like colleges with co-op programs that offer lots of career-oriented work opportunities for students while in college.

https://www.road2college.com/
colleges-with-coop-programs/

■ A very few colleges are tuition-free but often have limited program offerings.

https://www.usnews.com/education/best-
colleges/paying-for-college/articles/2012/06/12/
save-money-by-attending-tuition-free-colleges

■ Some colleges consider themselves nontraditional and offer unusual scheduling or program opportunities.

https://www.bestcolleges.com/blog/
nontraditional-colleges-and-universities/

■ This is a list of schools judged to be best for working students because of their scheduling flexibility.

https://www.collegerank.net/
best-colleges-for-working-students/

3. **WORK FOR A COMPANY WITH TUITION BENEFITS**: It may take you longer to complete your education while working and you may have to forego the experience of living on a college campus, but you can earn and learn at the same time.

https://thekrazycouponlady.com/tips/money/
11-companies-that-will-pay-for-your-college-degree

4. THINK ABOUT SCHOOLS THAT FIT CERTAIN CATEGORIES

- This list has schools judged to have the most student diversity.

  https://diverseeducation.com/article/53530/

- These are colleges judged to have exceptional impact on their students.

  https://ctcl.org/category/college-profiles/

- Here is a list of small innovative colleges.

  https://www.usnews.com/best-colleges/rankings/
  national-liberal-arts-colleges/innovative

- These 25 colleges have the best graduation rates:

  https://www.cbsnews.com/news/25-private-colleges-
  with-the-best-graduation-rates/

- If you are interested in going out-of-state but worried about cost, see these slides.

  https://www.usnews.com/education/best-colleges/
  slideshows/10-colleges-with-affordable-out-of-state-
  tuition?slide=13

- This is a list of schools especially interested in attracting First Generation students.

  https://imfirst.org/colleges/

5. **ONLINE OPTIONS**: You want more education, but your life is complicated and you cannot see how you can manage all your responsibilities and show up on a campus. Would online school be the right choice for you, at least for now?

   https://www.collegeconsensus.com/rankings/
   innovative-online-schools/

   https://www.collegeconsensus.com/features/
   online-community-college-guide/

6. **CANVAS YOUR IN-STATE OPTIONS:** Search online for ALL the schools in your state. Just type this in your browser: "All colleges in (name of state)" and you will get a list that gives you all schools in the state. When you click on the school name, the average tuition after aid, the percentage of students who graduate and the percent of applicants who are accepted show up.

   Are there schools you could reasonably reach by car/train/bus that might make sense for you that you did not think about?

When you are ready to decide where you will go to college, feel good knowing you have considered many choices, and you are fully informed about what kinds of financial aid you can access. And don't hesitate to negotiate over financial aid offers. You may not get a better deal, but often you can, especially if you have a better offer elsewhere to use as comparison. Going to college anywhere is a gift, but some gifts work better for us than others.

PRE-COLLEGE ADVICE FOR HIGH SCHOOL STUDENTS

1. https://www.usnews.com/education/scholarship-search-insider/articles/2018-02-15/4-organizations-First Generation-students-can-use-to-find-scholarships

2. https://www.collegexpress.com/scholarships/search

3. How to Choose a College: A Complete Guide—College Raptor

4. 33 Factors for How to Choose a College

5. How to decide if college is the right choice for you

6. 21 Easy-to-Follow Steps to Choosing the Right College in 2020

7. https://www.cappex.com/articles/blog/government-publishes-graduation-rate-data

8. https://www.bestvalueschools.com/rankings/colleges-First Generation-students/

9. https://www.usnews.com/education/best-colleges/articles/2019-05-14/what-you-should-know-as-a-First Generation-college-student

10. https://www.accreditedschoolsonline.org/resources/First Generation-college-students/

11. https://www.collegeconsensus.com/rankings/best-tuition-free-colleges/

12. https://www.niche.com/colleges/search/best-colleges-for-low-income/

13. https://www.greatschools.org/gk/articles/community-college-can-open-the-door-to-selective-universities/

APPENDIX III

WHO IS A FIRST GENERATION STUDENT?

FROM THE CENTER FOR FIRST GENERATION STUDENT SUCCESS

https://firstgen.naspa.org/blog/defining-First Generation

While the term "First Generation" may seem self-explanatory, the nuance of the identity does require examination. Often, First Generation students are categorized simply as those who are the first in their family to attend college. Yet, this leads to questions about the postsecondary experiences of extended family members, older siblings, and even non-family adults who have important roles in the lives of students. Many institutions have chosen to use the federal definition officially developed for TRIO program acceptance and to determine eligibility for Pell Grants which indicates First Generation students come from families where their biological parents did not complete a four-year college degree.

This leaves room for parents who may have attended some college, but did not complete, and college-going older siblings would be considered First Generation. There are also prevalent research definitions—one considering no parental education after high school and one considering no parental degree completion after high school. However, some institutions, and researchers, choose to remove the First Generation title from students with parents who have even once enrolled in a college course. More recently, some institutions have chosen to include students with parents who completed a four-year degree at an institution outside the United States as First Generation as well.

The definition has been found to vary across academic departments and programs at the same institution as well. A **November 2017 New York Times article** demonstrating the complexities of defining "First Gen" cited the work of University of Georgia professor, Robert K. Toutkoushian, who analyzed eight different versions of the term "First Generation." This research concluded that, across a sample of 7300 students, the number of students who could be defined as First Generation ranged from 22 percent to 77 percent. The recent renewed focus on First Generation student success has prompted many institutions to consider, or reconsider, how best to define "First Generation" and how it should subsequently be used in practice.

While defining First Gen may appear overwhelming and complicated, it is important to remember why it is important. Because identification as a First Generation college student is most often self-reported in the matriculation process, there are inherent gaps in the data. Moreover, by not having a definition, it is nearly impossible for an institution to identify these students, track their academic and co-curricular progress, pinpoint needs for early intervention, highlight successes, measure critically important learning outcomes, and benchmark against other institutions and national data sets.

Ultimately, the term "First Generation" implies the possibility that a student may lack the critical cultural capital necessary for college success because their parents did not attend college. While First Generation students are often quite academically skilled and contribute in many ways to a campus community, navigating the tangled web of college policies, procedures, jargon, and expectations can be a challenge. This pervasive "hidden curriculum" can damage the confidence of First Generation students, lead to struggles in belonging, and result in departure. This opens an opportunity for institutions to provide additional support for these students so they may be as competitive and successful as their peers.

GLOSSARY

Academic Probation—being on Academic Probation means that you have not been passing enough courses with at least a C or better. Even if your cumulative GPA is above 2.0, if your term GPA is between 1.5 and 1.9 (and you have been a student longer than one quarter) you will be on Academic Probation. Academic Probation is a warning that you have fallen into academic difficulty and that you need to improve your grades in order to reach "Good Standing" status to avoid risk of disqualification from the college or university.

Anxiety—a feeling of worry, nervousness, or unease, typically about an imminent event or something with an uncertain outcome. Anxiety is a normal emotion but can become abnormally heightened and is characterized by a state of excessive uneasiness and apprehension, typically with compulsive behavior or panic attacks.

Attention Deficit Disorder (ADD); (Also Attention Deficit/ Hyperactivity Disorder (ADHD)—ADD is a medical disorder that has symptoms of inattention, distractibility, and poor working memory. ADHD is the term used to describe additional symptoms of hyperactivity and impulsivity. It does not correlate with academic ability but can, if undiagnosed, hinder academic or work success.

Autism Spectrum Disorder—a neurological and developmental disorder that begins early in childhood and lasts throughout a person's life. It affects how a person acts and interacts with others, communicates, and learns. It includes what used to be known as Asperger Syndrome and pervasive developmental disorders.

Cornell Notes—the Cornell method provides a systematic format for condensing and organizing notes. This system of taking notes is designed for a high school or college level student.

Cultural Capital—the social assets (education, intellect, style of speech, style of dress, etc.) of a person that promote social mobility in a stratified society.

Curve—the process of adjusting student grades in order to ensure that a test or assignment has the proper distribution throughout the class (for example, only 20% of students receive A's, 30% receive B's, and so on), as well as a desired total average (for example, a C grade average for a given test)

Depression—a mood disorder that causes a persistent feeling of sadness and loss of interest and can interfere with your daily functioning.

Dyslexia—a general term for disorders that involve difficulty in learning to read or interpret words, letters, and other symbols, but that do not affect general intelligence. This is more prominent in males than females and may run in families.

Guilt—this is a feeling that comes from what we do that we believe is not good enough. It is a feeling based on our behavior.

Intimidation—1) to make timid; fill with fear. 2) to overawe or outrage, as through the force of personality or by a superior display of wealth, talent, etc.

Learn to learn—a focus on teaching strategies that enable the assimilation, understanding and retention of information.

Leave—this is a college-approved time-out from school that allows students to take a break from attending classes without formally withdrawing and eases the way into returning to studying.

Meditation—a practice where an individual uses a technique—such as mindfulness, or focusing the mind on a particular object, thought, or activity—to train attention and awareness, and achieve a mentally clear and emotionally calm and stable state.

Mentor—an experienced and trusted adviser. When students are able to work for a period of time with an experienced person who is willing to teach and coach them, it is known as a **mentorship**, often happening in the summer between college years.

Microaggression—a term used for brief and commonplace daily verbal, behavioral, or environmental indignities, whether intentional or unintentional, that communicate hostile, derogatory, or negative prejudicial slights and insults toward any group, particularly culturally marginalized groups.

Misogyny—dislike of, contempt for, or ingrained prejudice against women.

Networking—the action or process of interacting with others to exchange information and develop professional or social contacts.

Office Hours—faculty members are expected to set aside times each week meant for interacting with students. You may request time outside of office hours, but these specific hours are considered student time, and you are welcome to visit your teacher's office in this time frame. You may come to office hours with an interest or a problem, or you may come because you want to know your teacher better.

Plagiarism—when you borrow the words or key ideas directly from someone else who has presented them formally, usually in writing, and pretend they are your own with no reference to the original source, you are guilty of plagiarizing.

Protagonist—1) the leading character or one of the major characters in a drama, movie, novel, or other fictional text. 2) an advocate or champion of a particular cause or idea.

Racism—prejudice, discrimination, or antagonism directed against someone of a different race based on the belief that one's own race is superior.

References—1) something (such as a sign or indication) that refers a reader or consulter to another source of information (such as a book or passage). 2) a statement of the qualifications of a person seeking employment or appointment given by someone familiar with the person and often needed by college students for employment or graduate school admissions

Retention Rate—the percentage of a school's first-time, first-year undergraduate students who continue at that school the next year.

Shame—a feeling that grows out of the belief that we are not good enough. It is focused on us alone. It rests on our imagined self-image rather than on how we act in the world

Social Capital—a set of shared values that allows individuals in a group to work together effectively to achieve a common purpose.

Syllabus—an outline of a course. Most often it is handed out at the beginning of the semester. It usually tells students what the assignments are, what material will be covered in each class, when exams will be and what the expectations are. Office hours and faculty contact information are commonly found in the syllabus.

Synopsis—a brief summary of the major points of a subject or written work or story, either as prose or as a table; an abridgment or condensation of a work.

Transcript—in an academic context, this is the written summary of courses and grades and can usually be obtained from the school registrar.

TRIO—federal outreach and student services programs designed to identify and provide services for individuals from disadvantaged backgrounds. TRIO includes eight programs targeted to serve and assist low-income individuals, First Generation college students, and individuals with disabilities to progress through the academic pipeline from middle school to post-baccalaureate programs.

Unwritten Rules—behavioral constraints imposed in organizations or societies that are not voiced or written down. They usually exist in **unspoken** and **unwritten** format because they form a part of the logical argument or course of action implied by tacit assumptions.

Work-Study—is a school-based program that helps students with financial need find jobs on campus or sometimes in community organizations. Because the federal government contributes to the student's salary, it expands the number of jobs available.

ACKNOWLEDGMENTS

Much thanks to La'Shaye Cobley, who provided the spark that ignited this project.

This book is dedicated to all the First Generation students with whom I spoke—whose candor, thoughtfulness and generosity made it possible.

Our conversations have been a source of joy and motivation.

May this book bring inspiration and support to those on their college journey.

A special thanks to . . .

Pamela Long

Janet Christpeels

Ambar Lavenderos

Haliday Douglas

Nina Shmorhun

Juana Granados

Martha Berrera

Rob Gira

Shaya Kara

Tabreez Kara

Michelle Mullen

Jesse Meza

Stephen Kaufman

Ann Kaufman

Marc Lo

Ellen Cohen

Carolyn Truesdell

Sharon Owens

Beth Merfish

My applause to the book production team: Annie Preston, proofreader; and my ever-patient book designer, Karl Hunt.

Gratitude to Jesse Meza for volunteering a website and many discussions about how to put this book into the wide world.

Made in the USA
Coppell, TX
25 August 2022

82077564R00133